Do-It-Yourself Marriage Enrichment

Do-It-Yourself Marriage Enrichment

▼

A Workshop on Your Own Time, on Your Own Terms, on Your Own Turf

WARREN AND MARY EBINGER

ABINGDON PRESS

NASHVILLE

DO-IT-YOURSELF MARRIAGE ENRICHMENT
A Workshop on Your Own Time, on Your Own Terms, on Your Own Turf

This book is printed on acid-free paper.

Library of Congress Cataloging-in-Publication Data

Ebinger, Warren R.
    Do-it-yourself marriage enrichment : a workshop on your own time, on your own terms, on your own turf / Warren and Mary Ebinger.
      p. cm.
    Includes bibliographical references.
    ISBN 0-687-01039-X (paperback : alk. paper)
    1. Marriage—Religious aspects—Christianity. 2. Marriage counseling—United States. 3. Communication in marriage—United States. 4. Communication in the family—United States.
  I. Ebinger, Mary, 1929- . II. Title
  BV835.E323 1998
  248.8'44—dc21
                                  97-52048
                                    CIP

Unless otherwise noted, Scripture quotations are from the New Revised Standard Version Bible. Copyright © 1989 by the Division of Christian Education of the National Council of the Churches of Christ in the USA. Used by permission.

Scripture quotations marked CEV are from the *Contemporary English Version—New Testament:* Copyright © American Bible Society 1991.

Scripture quotations marked KJV are from the King James Version of the Bible.

FAMILY CIRCUS cartoon, page 138, by Bil Keane. Copyright 9/22/96. Reprinted with special permission of King Features Syndicate.

Suggestions, pages 82-83, from *1001 Ways to Be Romantic* by Gregory J. P. Godek. Copyright 1995 Gregory J. P. Godek, Casablanca Press.

"Ten Steps for Resolving Couple Conflict," pages 169-70. Permission to use this model was provided by Life Innovations. The Ten Steps for Resolving Couple Conflict is a component in the PREPARE/ENRICH Program that was developed by Dr. David H. Olson, who is Professor, Family Social Science, University of Minnesota, St. Paul, Minnesota.

"Juggling Act Inventory," pages 29-31. Reprinted with permission from *Structured Exercises in Stress Management, Volume 1,* copyright 1983, 1994. Donald A Tubesing. Published by Whole Person Associates Inc, 210 West Michigan, Duluth, MN 55802-1908, 218-727-0500.

Prayer, page 38, from *Deep Is the Hunger* by Howard Thurman. Copyright 1951 Howard Thurman, Prinit Press, Dublin, Indiana. Used by permission of Howard Thurman Educational Trust.

98 99 00 01 02 03 04 05 06 07—10 9 8 7 6 5 4 3 2 1

MANUFACTURED IN THE UNITED STATES OF AMERICA

To those couples

who have participated in our marriage retreats

we have counseled before marriage and those during their married lives in which healing took place

with whom we have shared in their weddings and hopes for the future

and

our dear married children, Lee and Gary, Lori and Greg, Jonathan and Mary Louise

CONTENTS

▼

PREFACE

▼

It was a warm, sunny day when we celebrated our first wedding anniversary. We decided to review our marriage. How could we improve? What was happening in our lives—our schedules, our finances, our work, our goals, our spiritual lives? This review then became an annual event. Through the years, our marriage has been an exciting, beautiful adventure as we have continued working to improve it, adapt it, and keep it vital.

Through the years, in our roles as a pastoral counselor and a minister of various churches, we have helped many couples prepare for marriage and handle concerns and problems at different times of their lives. Marriage enrichment weekends, workshops, and seminars have been a part of this expanding "circle of love." This book comes out of those experiences and our own marriage of more than forty years. Our three children, Lee, Lori, and Jonathan; their mates, Gary, Greg, and Mary Louise; and our dear grandchildren, Elizabeth, Caroline, and Katie have added a joyful, loving, and refreshing quality to our family circle of love.

God's creative Spirit has continued to permeate our relationship as husband and wife in ways that we never could have imagined. We thank God for our lives together.

INTRODUCTION

▼

Would you like to enrich and strengthen your marriage but are unable to attend a marriage workshop or marriage enrichment weekend? If so, this book is for you. This "do-it-yourself" marriage enrichment "workshop" will help you explore and improve your marriage relationship at your own pace and on your own terms. Whether or not you've ever attended a marriage workshop or enrichment experience, you will find the exercises in this book both meaningful and fun.

How long have you been married? It doesn't matter. Any couple is able to grow in the process of exploring their relationship in this way. Do you have children? If so, you will find specific help related to this important aspect of your relationship in chapter 8. If not, simply skip that chapter. Have you been married previously? Is yours a "blended" family? This book also considers your unique situations and needs.

When can you find time in your busy schedule to focus on your marriage? Be creative. The first year we were married, we bicycled (we had no car!) to a park to take an "inventory" of our marriage. After that, the "inventory" became an annual event. Some years we talked on Sunday afternoons when the children were asleep. At other times, we took a picnic or went out for dinner and talked about our marriage. Occasionally, we went away for a weekend by ourselves to examine our life together. You will think of other ways and times when you can focus on your marriage relationship. Perhaps you will want to explore your marriage during a weekend, or pace your exploration over a period of weeks or months. Perhaps you are part of a church group or circle of friends who might use this book for several weeks, focusing on one chapter at a time and sharing only as you are comfortable.

Whatever method you choose, each of you will find it helpful to have a notebook or journal on hand. Space has been provided in the book for those exercises that are to be completed as a couple. Exercises that are to be completed individually and then shared and discussed may be recorded in your notebooks, along with any notes you would like to record for future reference.

There are several keys to a successful do-it-yourself marriage enrichment workshop. First, make it fun! We've tried to include creative ideas related to where, when, and even how the exercises in this book may be completed. You will think of other ways to make this an enjoyable experience. Second, don't try to cover too much at once—even if your time is limited to a weekend. Take one chapter at a time, allowing time for reflection in between. Third, listen to each other and try to be as objective as possible. And finally, be loving toward each other as you explore your "circle of love" and grow closer together.

What is your "circle of love"? It is God's plan for your marriage, joining two individuals as one. Just as a circle is unending, symbolizing wholeness, completeness, and fullness, your circle of love binds you together in God's perfect, unending love. That's what this book is all about—helping you to focus your attention on your circle of love and, with God's help, to strengthen it. Christ's instruction to "love one another" means that we are to love each other *unconditionally.* For couples, this does not mean that we should not work toward positive change in our relationship or discover how to grow in our marriage; rather, it means we should focus on changing *ourselves*—not on changing our spouse.

If you have serious problems in your marriage or discover them as you make your way through the book, seek professional counseling. This book is not intended to be a "quick fix" for marital problems, but a tool to help you give attention to some important areas of your marriage that often are neglected in day-to-day living.

Bathing the whole process in prayer is important. Before beginning your workshop and at the beginning of each time together, take time to pray. This will set the tone for your exploration together. Brief devotional thoughts, including scripture and prayer, are included throughout the book. If you remain open to God and to each other, God will help you improve your marriage and will enrich it more than you can possibly imagine.

Remember, as Wilfred L. Peterson says in *The Art of Marriage,*

> It is not only marrying the right partner,
> It is being the right partner.

Warren and Mary

1. THE CIRCLE OF LOVE
▼

The August day started out warm and a little rainy. Judy's zipper on her simple, long white wedding dress had separated the day before when she tried it on. Why didn't she think of having someone check it? There just wasn't time. Thankfully, the zipper locked and stayed! She did not want to think about what would happen if it hadn't! Her short hair, with its curls, was tucked under a lace cap.

She was happy and trembling with excitement. She thought sadly for a moment about her father, who had died during her first year in college, and about her brother, who could not be there. She looked down the aisle of the church, held her flowers tightly, and wondered if she could walk alone as she had planned to do. (Her new shoes were a little tight!) Then Judy saw Tim, his brown eyes full of love, and as she looked at him, her unsteady feet found their way to him. She tucked her arm in his and knew that their lives together would be beautiful.

Tim had driven hurriedly down the country roads from his farm home that day, after picking up the punch and cake for the simple reception they had planned at the church. He arrived in the rented car at the door of the church, barely making it on time. He took the punch to the basement and hurried up to the sanctuary. The organist began the piece he knew was his cue. From the front of the church, Tim looked at Judy and her glowing face and thought about their future together.

As they said their memorized vows, "For better, for worse, in health and sickness, for richer, for poorer, as long as we both shall live," he looked lovingly at Judy.

Then came her words, "Tim, I give you this ring as a sign of my unending love." Judy took the ring and tried to put it on his right hand. When he pulled gently away, she looked questioningly at him and then realized her mistake. She placed the ring on his left hand as they smiled at each other, almost laughing.

Kneeling at the altar after communion, while the Lord's Prayer was being sung, Judy and Tim realized God was blessing their marriage.

1. Looking at Our Circle of Love

Devotional Thought: What is love? Read 1 Corinthians 13 aloud together, perhaps alternating verses, and then reading together, "And now faith, hope, and love abide, . . . and the greatest of these is love."

Prayer: Lord, thank you for our marriage. Help us to grow closer together and to you as we explore our relationship. Be with us now. Amen.

A circle never ends. It is whole, complete. The wedding ring symbolizes unending love. God plans for your marriage to be a circle of love.

On a wedding day, there is usually a family circle, who look at the couple and remember when the two of them were children. It is hard for them to believe that this little boy and girl have changed so much and are ready for a life together. A circle of friends surround the couple as well. And God's enveloping love also encircles them.

When God is at the center of your circle of love, sorrow, sickness, and difficult times cannot break the circle. Through good and bad, God helps to strengthen and sustain your marriage and enrich your lives. If you look at your marriage under the light of God's love as you explore together during this time, your love will deepen and grow. Frequently the thirteenth chapter of 1 Corinthians is read at a wedding, describing the qualities of God's love. These qualities can be applied to the way you relate through love in your marriage.

At the time of your wedding, you took vows, exchanged rings, and most likely, celebrated the occasion with family and friends. It was a very special day, one you will never forget. Yet as you go through the everyday experiences of life, your memories of this special day can fade. This is why it can be very meaningful to look back on your wedding day—to visualize it again, to cherish the beginning of your relationship as husband and wife, to laugh at the little things that may have gone wrong and seemed more important then, and especially to remember the vows you took.

Take a few minutes to reflect on your wedding day. Did the sun shine? Where did you have the ceremony? Were there many guests or just a few friends? Who was there? Do you remember the flowers? How did you feel before—and after—the ceremony? Did you have a simple reception in a church hall or a large one in a hotel or garden? Did anything humorous happen? What is most meaningful to you about your memories?

Remembering your wedding can be a delightful way to begin looking at your circle of love. Did you have a wedding or unity candle when you were married? Perhaps you might like to light a candle now and look at your wedding pictures or video as you think about the beginning of your marriage. Here are some questions you might reflect on. As you talk, you might like to have cake and coffee together.

Reflecting on Our Wedding Day

▲ What was the day like? Cold? Sunny? Windy? Did it matter?

▲ Who was there? What friends came from a distance? Was someone missing we really wanted to be there?

▲ What were some of the most meaningful parts of the ceremony? The vows? The music?

▲ Was there anything we would have changed? Can we accept it now, even if everything was not perfect?

▲ What words said then do we need especially to remember to make the rest of our marriage even more meaningful?

You might end your time of sharing by saying your vows again. If you don't remember them, perhaps you have a videotape of your wedding or a printed copy of the ceremony (many ministers give these to couples). Then you might kneel together—perhaps in candlelight—or simply clasp your hands together and say a prayer, such as this one:

Lord, we remember our wedding and our vows. Be with us now as we share together and think about how we can continually renew our marriage. Thank you for the times ahead when we will talk about our circle of love. In Jesus' name, who taught us how to truly love. Amen.

Take a moment now to set another time when you will explore the priorities in your circle of love.

Devotional Thought: In Matthew 6:21, Jesus says, "Where your treasure is, there your heart will be also." What are your priorities? You might begin by reading Matthew 6:19-21. As you explore your priorities, you might want to have a wedding picture or other picture of the two of you within view, symbolizing the priority of your marriage. You also might light a candle to represent the light of Christ shining and guiding your lives together.

Prayer: Lord, thank you for our circle of love. Guide us now as we look at the priorities in our lives and in our marriage. We ask in Jesus' name. Amen.

2. Priorities in the Circle

Judy looked at Tim. It seemed that his job was more important than her or the children. He worked long hours for his company and often did not arrive home until late in the evening. She wanted the family to eat together, but this seldom happened. Then, too, the work she took home seemed to be a continual block to their communication and a source of considerable tension. *Why am I doing this?* she asked herself. *Why are we doing this?*

It seemed that everything was a vicious circle—rather than a happy, fulfilling, or creative circle. Even the children could sense the stress. They seemed to be moving farther away from Judy and Tim.

"I love you, Tim," Judy sobbed one Sunday night, when Tim's head finally came to rest on the pillow beside her. He turned out the light after switching off the lap computer he had focused on for the last forty minutes, preparing a report for the stockholders' meeting the next day.

"Uh huh," muttered Tim sleepily. He always seemed to fall asleep so suddenly, as if his whole system shut down when the computer was turned off.

"Tim, don't you hear me?" Judy questioned in a tired, weepy little voice. She ran her fingers through his wavy black hair the way she used to years ago, when Sunday nights were relaxed and lips were moist and kisses were a communication all their own.

"Tim, how can you just fall asleep when I need you, when I want to talk, when things seem to be coming apart in our lives, when even the children know that we're not close like we used to be? We're too busy with our work, with everything outside our circle. Tim, do you hear me? Can we talk?"

Tim thought to himself that when he tried to get close to Judy, she was often too busy with the children, or too tired. He shifted his body, turned onto his right side—his usual sleeping position—and replied in a muffled voice, speaking into his pillow, "I'm so sleepy, honey. Let's talk tomorrow."

It was always "tomorrow." Judy cried softly. Her pillow was wet with tears. The clock struck twelve.

What happened in Tim and Judy's marriage occurs ever so gradually in many marriages. It is a matter of priorities. Values are juggled along with jobs, children, and other responsibilities. Never enough time. Never enough money. Why?

There are no easy answers, and there's no turning back the clock. That's why it is so important for couples to determine their priorities early in their relationship—even before they marry, if possible—and to continually review and revise them as necessary. Still, it's never too late for couples to "get their priorities straight," whether they currently are sailing on smooth waters or are experiencing one of the mild "storms" that rock even the strongest of relationships from time to time. How do you begin?

As suggested in the preceding devotional thought, you might use a lighted candle and a photograph of the two of you as symbols as you explore your priorities, or you could go to a restaurant or park to continue the process. A different surrounding often lends more objectivity and fun to this kind of exercise. Take this book with you, along with notebooks and pencils.

What are your priorities? Career? Children? Each other? Where does God fit into the picture? In the pages that follow, you will continue the story of Tim and Judy as you attempt to answer these questions. You will see that, for them, the key was agreeing to spend time alone together so that they could reprioritize their lives and enhance their relationship.

The secret of your own success in this effort lies in your willingness to enter into a process of wide-open, nonjudgmental exploration of each other, of yourselves, and of your values and priorities, followed by experimentation—which, of course, involves risk and vulnerability. Taking steps into your circle of love requires that you *spend time together* focusing on the priorities that are presently in place—whether intentionally or not—and those that could be structured into a future relationship.

Judy and Tim's circle looked like this:

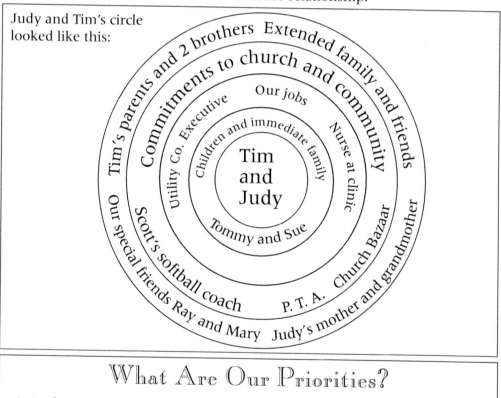

What Are Our Priorities?

1. In the circle of priorities write your names in the center.

2. In the concentric circles around the inner circle, write your other commitments, such as your jobs, community and church involvement, and extended family and friends.

3. Then talk about the different priorities in your marriage.

Your circle of priorities:

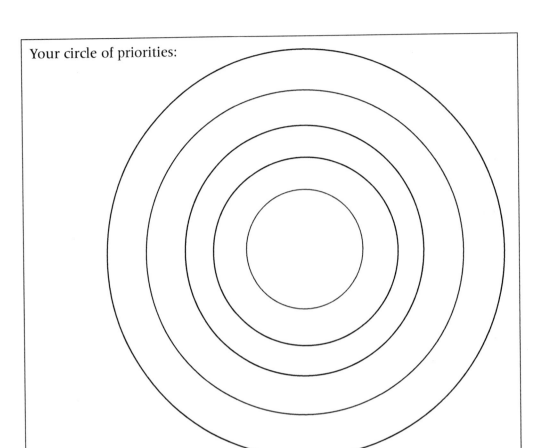

4. Now focus on the inner circle, representing your marriage relationship. On another piece of paper, each of you draw just that circle, listing what you consider to be top priorities in your marriage—not necessarily in any order.

Judy's circle looked like this:

Tim and Judy
Enough money for
daily needs and savings
Caring for our children
Good meals—clean house
Health
Really talking with Tim
Caring for my mother
Growing spiritually
People who need me
(at the clinic)

Tim's circle looked looked like this:

Tim and Judy
Family needs
Security on my job
Keeping everyone healthy
Saving for kids' college
House maintenance/repair
Time for Judy and me
Making a difference in
the world!
Sports

5. Share your lists, explaining what they mean to each of you. Recognize that each of you may have listed different priorities and may have forgotten some that the other person included. Allow enough time to talk about these, accepting the differences and realizing that the combined priorities represent your marriage at this moment.

The inner circle, which represents your marriage, is—or should be—most important, at least in terms of your relationship. It is the circle of love. It is where you have to be if you are married, however imperfect. Just as the wedding ring symbolizes a circle of unending love, so the inner circle identifies you with someone else in a covenant, which is inclusive of the two of you.

Close this time together with a prayer, such as this:

> Lord, help us to understand your words when you said, "Strive first for the kingdom . . . and all these things will be given to you as well" (Matthew 6:33). May our priorities be your priorities, and help us to accept each other's opinions in love. Amen.

Decide the time and place you will continue your exploration of your marriage. Perhaps you might decide on a picnic at the park—when the children, if you have any, are in school or are staying with grandparents or a baby-sitter, so that you can have uninterrupted time. Or you could spend a night away in a hotel that features special weekend rates. If not, you might plan a quiet evening together, with a late night dinner after the children are tucked in bed. Spend some time relaxing together before you begin.

3. Our Marriage Inventory

Devotional Thought:
"For the LORD is good;
his steadfast love endures forever,
and his faithfulness to all generations" (Psalm 100:5).
Think for a moment about how good God is to you and how God's love surrounds you as you love each other.

Prayer: Dear God, thank you for accepting us and help us now to accept each other and grow together. In Jesus' name we pray. Amen.

It is helpful to take an inventory of your marriage, not to work on solving any problems but to see the total picture. In this way you will be able to gradually understand the ways in which your individual hopes and dreams, as well as your feelings and frustrations, relate to your marriage relationship and help to define specific areas you will want to explore together.

Such a process should involve fun as well as serious reflection. Keep in mind that within your circle of love there are always possibilities for new awareness, which eventually leads to celebrating your differences as well as your "oneness."

Taking Inventory

1. On separate sheets of paper, each of you draw a large circle and label it "My Inventory of Our Marriage."
2. Divide the circle into four quadrants, labeling them with the following headings to represent your feelings about your marriage:

What I Like Most Now	What I Like Least Now
Past Values/Experiences Now Missing	Future Values/Experiences Desired

3. Now complete your lists individually, making them honest and open.

4. After you complete your circles, take a brief break for a walk or some refreshments, so that when you come together again you can look objectively at the four quadrants.

Before looking at your inventories, look at what the circles of Tim and Judy revealed. Take turns reading their lists.

"What I Like Most Now"

Tim's list:
Hot breakfasts together
TV news and sports
Camping with Judy and the
  children
Working in the garden together

Judy's list:
Going out to dinner
Talking together
Surprise gifts (little or big)
Walking together on a cool evening
Tucking the kids in bed together

"What I Like Least Now"

Tim's list:

Constant repair and maintenance
of home/lawn
Arguments with Judy
Concerns/disagreement about
discipline of children
Telephone calls from colleagues
or Judy's family
Missing socks
Children always wanting things
they don't need

Judy's list:

Disagreements at any time of day
especially in the morning
Paying bills
Trying to balance the checkbook
Hurried meals
Stacks of dishes or laundry
Tim arriving home later than promised
The computer claiming so much of
Tim's time

"Past Values/Experiences Now Missing"

Tim's list:

Singing in the church choir
Playing racquet ball together
Biking together
Making pancakes on Saturday
Playing with the children
Attending sports events together
Playing Scrabble and doing
crossword puzzles together
Going to the movies

Judy's list:

Relaxed lovemaking
More help from Tim with household
tasks
Surprise flowers
Little love notes
Going to church together
Listening to classical music together
Reading the newspaper together
Kisses and hugs at unexpected times

"Future Values/Experiences Desired"

Tim's list:

Joining a health club and
swimming as a family once a
week
Hiking with the family
Attending church regularly as
a family
Reading poetry together
Taking a computer course together
and getting on line with Internet

Judy's list:

Romantic weekend away while
grandparents care for children
Share more cooking responsibilities
Planning the week's activities,
including children's needs
Investing in answering machine
Joining church study fellowship group
Eating out once a week
Interviewing for less demanding job
Redecorating bedroom together

Now read your lists aloud with tenderness. This will require some patience in simply listening to each other. The items under "What I Like Most" may need some interpretation, and those under "What I Like Least" will need to be carefully explained and understood. For instance, here's a conversation that might take place between Tim and Judy if they were not gentle or patient with each other:

Judy: Tim, how can you possibly say you like "hot breakfasts together" when you never allow time for breakfast? You are always hurrying, saying you'll be late for work!

Tim: Judy, I can't believe you said "walking together on a cool evening" is what you like most. As I recall, you say you're always too tired to go anywhere at night!

Neither of these quick responses would be helpful. Tim and Judy need to recognize that though these "like most" experiences are infrequent, they are very special. It is so important to consider the other person's expression of equal importance when sharing the responses under "What I Like Least."

When dealing with "Past Values/Experiences Now Missing," look creatively at what this means. Is it possible to include this past value or experience in the present (e.g., writing love notes) even if this is a different time of life (e.g., having children at home to nurture)?

Again, allow plenty of time to share these feelings of past, present, and future. At the same time, do not let yourselves get "stuck" in one area or discouraged with the process. The ability to clarify some of these inner feelings about yourself and your marriage will be most helpful as you prepare to take the next step: prioritizing.

After you have shared your responses as fully as possible, take a look at the following comments of Tim and Judy. Perhaps you would like to read these aloud as dialogue, assuming the roles of Tim and Judy and expressing with emotion the words they are speaking to each other. Have fun with it, and perhaps you will gain a few insights for your own relationship.

Tim: You know what? We're more alike than I thought in terms of what we want in life! How come we're often on different wave lengths, or so it seems?

Judy: We just don't take time to share, I guess. We're always too busy with our work, trying to get ahead of the game, never really reviewing what we've done or planning what should be next. I think so much of it is wrapped up in paychecks.

Tim: Are you really worried about money, Judy?

Judy: Sure I am, Tim. It's probably a higher priority than I even realize.

Tim: Why?

Judy: Because I'm continually afraid something will happen to you—you travel so much lately. If not an accident, a heart attack or cancer or something else.... *(voice starting to waver)*

Tim: What is it, Judy?

Judy: I'm scared, Tim, because I couldn't handle life with the children all by myself. And I'm afraid there wouldn't be enough money. I guess it all goes back to my parents, especially my mother's constant concern about having enough money for our education, for the mortgage, and so many other things.

Tim: Maybe I should take out more term life insurance, to care for you and the kids for the next fifteen years if something should happen to me.

Judy: Don't talk that way—about something happening to you. I don't want to think about it that way.

Tim: But *you* brought it up. It was *your* concern about me not being here to pay the bills. What do you want me to do?

Judy: Well, you might start by getting a physical. Remember how your dad died at 45 from a heart attack? Maybe it runs in the family.

Tim: Okay. I'll make an appointment this week with Dr. Jamison. I think I'm beginning to understand something. I've just never realized before that even though you're a very independent person, for which I'm grateful, you are still very dependent on me. It makes me feel good, in a way, that you need me, not only for making ends meet but for making life good. And you know what, Judy? I'm more dependent on you than you probably can imagine. Just to know that you are part of my life, that you do so many things that make life good and joyful, makes me happy. If anything ever happened to you, I'd be lost. I really need you. Why haven't I said that more often? Why haven't I told you that by bringing home flowers or taking time to linger over a late dinner, or staying awake while in bed at night, to discover the deep joy of simply holding you close?

Judy: Oh, Tim, don't blame yourself. I'm just as much at fault for not expressing what I feel and not taking time to share all of myself with you. I'm glad we had this talk. I feel we're at a point of a new beginning in our marriage. As you used to say when we were first married, "the honeymoon isn't over yet!"

Tim: Right! But have we overlooked one important thing in all this?

Judy: What's that?

Tim: God.

Judy: What do you mean?

Tim: We both listed church as a need or value in our lives. Have we been overlooking something important in our lives—something that gives us power or strength beyond ourselves? I've never been as good at expressing this as you have, Judy, but I feel an emptiness inside now that we're not going to church regularly. I guess I've thought I could go it alone too much of the time lately.

Judy: So have I, Tim. And I didn't realize you missed church as much as I did. So when you started jogging and doing yard work and household repairs on Sunday mornings, I slipped into a routine of doing laundry and paying the bills.

Tim: Well, at least you watched a church service on television while you were writing the checks. That's more than I did.

Judy: That's probably why I couldn't get the checkbook to balance. I never could do two things at once! And besides, it just proved to me that you can't really take time away from worship to handle financial matters.

I'll never forget the minister at our home church saying, "Where your treasure is, there will your heart be also." Maybe that is the key to just about everything!

Tim: Remember how we used to pray with the kids at every meal and at night, kneeling at the bed with them when they were little? When have we prayed together lately?

Judy: How about now, Tim?

Time to take a break and prepare to shift focus to the final "circle" of this chapter.

4. Our Priorities for the Future

> **Devotional Thought:** How do you decide what you want to do together as you look to the future? Read together Matthew 7:7: "Ask, and it will be given you; search, and you will find; knock, and the door will be opened for you."
>
> **Prayer:** Creative and loving God, help us as we plan for the future to place first things first in our lives, as Christ guides us. Amen.

As you take a look together at what you have learned about your marriage, about yourselves, and about your values and priorities, it is important to establish which priorities you agree should be the focus for your future. List all of these priorities in the circle provided. Be sure to look over the first "priorities circles" you drew (see p. 16) and those from the inventory (see p. 18). These will provide the basis for your creative decision making. Do not exclude any priorities that you feel strongly about, on the basis that they are "impractical." Remember, this is a "working document."

Look at the entire process as a growth experience and the basis for communication, change, and compromise along the way. If you're wondering what to do with the concentric circles you developed at the beginning of your exploration (pp. 15-16), hold on to these for now. We will look at how your newly agreed upon inner circle of priorities relates to the surrounding circles of immediate family, jobs, community, and extended family/friends when we take a look at the challenges of "Juggling Day by Day" in chapter 2.

What if one of you does not agree with what the other wants to list? Talk it through with the goal of making a decision that embraces both of you, as symbolic of your faith and love in and for God and each other. That is not easy, yet it *can* be fun. Laugh about some of your struggles in reaching agreement. Perhaps make a separate list of the items you need to discuss further before placing them inside the circle.

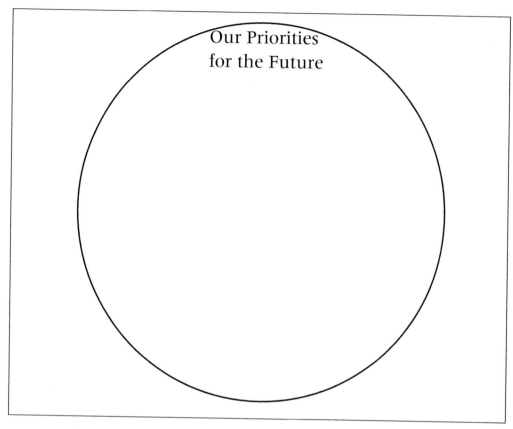

Our Priorities
for the Future

Remember, all that you have done thus far forms the basis for an adventure into the next chapter of this book and of your marriage. None of us has a perfect marriage, nor will we ever. However, *all* of us can improve and enhance the experience of sharing life as husband and wife.

Remember also that the "turnaround" that happened so quickly for Tim and Judy is not likely to occur all at once for you. In fact, it is very unlikely. The "quick fix" is what most of us want in resolving any marital difficulties or in reestablishing communication with a high level of trust and fulfillment. Yet these goals can be realized only through a longer commitment of time. Although it is ideal to review your priorities in a setting that is not cluttered with other responsibilities or distractions, this is not always possible. Priorities relate to everyday life and must be considered "all along the way." Even so, it is still necessary for you periodically to schedule time together when you can be away from the clutter. Take your calendar out and agree on a date now!

Establishing priorities is only the beginning. The remainder of this book will give specifics about how to live out your decisions and use them to strengthen and improve your circle of love. One word that will continue to be part of this focus is "hope." It will permeate everything we explore in this book and in the life experiences that are part of the ongoing venture of marriage. *Hope* is the key to almost everything. It is that inner feeling that there is something good awaiting us if we trust God to guide and bless us along the way. Hope is the connecting link between faith and love, as the apostle Paul defines it: "Faith, hope, and love abide." It is a critical component in every fulfilling marriage. When hope is present, there is also a sense of peace, as the following words from the hymn "O Master Let Me Walk with Thee" remind us. Let this be a closing prayer that you share together:

> In hope that sends a shining ray
> far down the future's broadening way,
> in peace that only thou canst give,
> with thee, O Master, let me live. Amen.

2. JUGGLING DAY BY DAY

▼

Dan and Maria have been married for almost five years. Their priorities center on being successful in their careers, taking care of their daughter, Kristen, maintaining a comfortable home, relating to their larger family circle as time permits, and trying to help in the church and community. They would describe themselves as being very much in love, yet continually frustrated by too much to do.

It is Friday night, as Dan and Maria are concluding a busy week and looking forward to Saturday. Dan is in the shower as he calls out to Maria, who is brushing her teeth.

"How about a weekend away to celebrate our fifth anniversary next month? Does that sound good to you, Maria? Where would you like to go?"

"Dan, are you serious? We've got too much going on this summer, with my mother coming and getting our place fixed up—and all the expenses that go with it. Why do you always get these ideas when you're in the shower? I'd rather discuss plans when we're not rushed, when I can see you as we're talking."

"You can see me now," Dan says, sliding open the shower door. "Could you throw me a towel?"

"What if I say no?"

"Well, then I guess I'll just have to step out and give you a hug while I'm all wet." And that's exactly what he does.

"Dan, you're getting my nigh-t-ie all w-e-t." Her words are muffled by the warm, wet kiss that seems to melt away any other thoughts.

"You wanted to wear another one tonight anyway, didn't you?"

A half hour later, Maria does put on another nightie.

The next day is Saturday. Saturday mornings are always a little more relaxed. Maria looks up at Dan as she pours her second cup of coffee and reaches for another bagel, which is part of their Saturday ritual. Dan had picked them up at the donut shop on the way home from his usual two-mile run.

"You know, Dan, the idea of an anniversary weekend that you splashed into my thoughts from the shower last night does sound kind of neat, if we could arrange it. But you can't expect me to say yes right away when I'm not even on the same wavelength. You always seem to get romantic ideas in the shower, and I'm taken by surprise on the outside."

"Maybe you should come in with me. Our shower's big enough, you know."

"Dan, you're irresistible at times, and so are your ideas, but you don't seem to realize how much planning goes into even a weekend away, especially now that we have to make arrangements for Kristen! Who is going to want to take care of a three-year-old for a whole weekend?"

"How about your mother? Couldn't she stay with Kristen? We could schedule our time away during her visit."

"My mother probably would think we shouldn't leave Kristen with anyone. She and my dad never got away even for a few days when my brother and I were little!"

"Well, we're not your mother and dad, Maria! We're us. This is our life."

"Okay, Dan, but I just don't feel right asking her to help us when nobody did this for her. Besides, the week she'll be with us is her vacation from her job. On the other hand, maybe she *would* like to spend some time alone with Kristen."

Maria reaches for her spiral calendar which she takes with her everywhere. It is bulging with several sheets of paper. One falls out.

"What's that?" Dan asks. "Looks like a list."

"It's a list of all the things we should be doing this weekend."

"Sometimes you make too many lists, Maria."

"It's the only way I get things done," she replies a little defensively.

"But it makes me feel as if we never *will* get everything done," Dan says. "Sometimes I think that when I get to heaven, you'll be waiting there with a list for me."

"You sound pretty confident that you're getting into heaven, and that I'm going there first," Maria said slightly annoyed.

"I'm just kidding, honey. The fact is, though, I know you'll be there, whatever it's like. You're a lot more religious than I am."

"Let's talk about *that* sometime," Maria replied as she reached out for Dan's strong, warm hand. "I love you, Dan, but I feel we are trying to crowd too much into our lives right now. We're just too busy. Our marriage is too busy! We try to do too many things without enough time to enjoy each other and Kristen. Uh oh, I hear her calling. It's time to get her up. Can you get out the cereal she likes, and put half a bagel on her plate? Let's talk more later."

Do-It-Yourself Marriage Enrichment

1. Our Day-by-Day Juggling Act

Devotional Thought: "This is the day that the LORD has made; let us rejoice and be glad in it" (Psalm 118:24).

How do you start the day? Happy? Thankful? Sometimes it may be difficult. It is important to realize that each day is good and that sharing life is a privilege, even when there is too much to do. The psalmist continually focused on the need to be thankful to God.

Prayer: Lord, thank you for this day. As we think about the many things we have to do every day, we thank you for each moment we have in life. Help us to celebrate this moment, the *now,* this time together here, to enjoy and explore the paths we take as we juggle our days alone and together. In Jesus' name, Amen.

How do you feel about your day-by-day schedule? Is it too full? Just right? Do you like the way you see yourselves? Are you worried about getting everything done? Talk together for just a few minutes (about five at most). Don't try to come up with solutions right now.

Juggling is something few of us are able to master with any degree of proficiency, whether it be three or more balls or saucers in the air at the same time. In a marriage, "juggling" is something all of us must do. And surprisingly, we can juggle more than we might think, if we try to do so with a creative spirit and realistic expectations.

In many ways, juggling follows our decisions about *priorities*. What we determine to do within the "circle of love" needs to fit into a pattern of manageable activities without causing us too much stress.

Let's look into the life of Maria and Dan again. It is still Saturday morning. Coffee cups are empty. Kristen has finished breakfast and is watching her favorite television program in the family room. Dan and Maria are still in the kitchen. Read the following conversation as dialogue, assuming their roles and putting expression into their words.

Dan: Are we becoming workaholics or what? Shouldn't there be a time for *us?* What's happened. It wasn't like this in the beginning.

Maria: Probably we've just tackled too much at once, or maybe we're in a rut, thinking we can't change anything. You're in city planning, Dan. Why don't you come up with some answers?

Dan: I think marriage planning is sometimes tougher to manage than city planning. *(Pauses)* But you know, there may be something that could help us. It was on my boss's desk a couple of weeks ago. He told me to take a copy. I almost forgot about it. Let's see if it's still in my briefcase. *(Pauses)* Yes, here it is. This might really help us, Maria. It's called "The Juggler." Did you ever see a real juggler?

Maria: Only once, when I was with my parents at a carnival. I was a little girl then.

Dan: I actually knew a guy who could juggle balls, dishes, knives. He was really good at it—hardly ever dropped any. He kept it up as a hobby in college. After a while he was even juggling flaming torches—still an amateur, but working his way through graduate school.

Maria: Did you ever try it?

Dan: A couple of times, but I couldn't get the knack of it. You really have to be skillful and quick, yet look relaxed at the same time.

Maria: Let's see *you* try it. I've got some tennis balls right here in the closet.

Maria returns with three balls and tosses them to Dan. He is able to juggle two, but continually drops them all when trying three.

Maria then tries, with little success, and all three balls roll from the kitchen into the living room. Both race over to pick them up. Maria pulls Dan to the floor with her and they roll over together, wrapping their arms around each other for a moment, their lips touching.

Kristen calls from the family room, asking for a glass of juice. Dan and Maria get up quickly and pour juice for themselves and for Kristen, who is still watching television. Coming back to the kitchen, they continue their conversation. (Continue reading the dialogue aloud, again taking their roles.)

Dan: We ought to play more! When was the last time we rolled around on the living room floor like that?

Maria: It's been a while, Danny! Now, what's this thing called "The Juggler"?

Dan: Here it is. The idea is to write in the little circles what we're juggling—what we're trying to keep up in the air, what we've dropped, and what we want to pick up.

Maria: Okay. Let's try it.

Dan: I don't know if I'm really into this right now, Maria. I probably shouldn't have suggested this whole idea. The lawn has to be mowed. I've got bushes to trim, and my car should be washed. We're too busy today.

Maria: I guess you're right. Saturday's the day to keep up with everything around here. How about tomorrow night? Could we do it then?

Dan: You mean "juggle"?

Maria: Yes, with this (*holding up the paper*).

Dan: Okay. It's a deal.

Dan and Maria kept their Sunday night commitment. Before looking at their juggling attempts, check out your own feelings about juggling. Are you both willing to give it a try?

Making the decision to take time to look at how life is going for each of you is the key. What's *really* happening day by day?

Just for Fun . . .

1. Find three small balls (tennis balls, little rubber balls, or other small unbreakable objects).
2. Start by trying to juggle one, then two, then all three, if possible. Be prepared to feel awkward!
3. Be ready to laugh. Cheer each other on.
4. Be sure both of you try this, regardless of the results. See if you can improve your skill in just a few moments.

Before you begin to look at what's happening in your day-by-day life experience of juggling, focus on why you are doing this exercise. What is at the center of this effort? Who is ready to help you?

Devotional Thought: Read aloud these words from Matthew 11:28-29: "Come to me, all you that are weary and are carrying heavy burdens, and I will give you rest. Take my yoke upon you, and learn from me."

Prayer: Spend a moment in silent prayer.

Now take a look at the juggling acts of Maria and Dan. What have they managed to keep up in the air and what have they dropped?

Maria's Juggling Act—

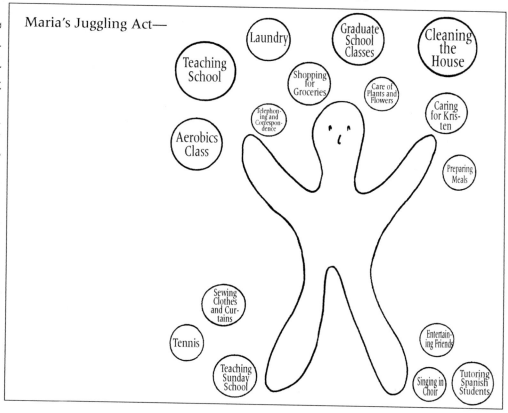

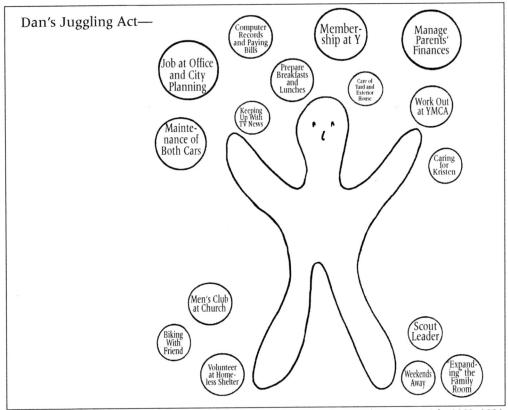

Dan's Juggling Act—

Computer Records and Paying Bills

Member-ship at Y

Manage Parents' Finances

Job at Office and City Planning

Prepare Breakfasts and Lunches

Care of Yard and Exterior House

Work Out at YMCA

Keeping Up With TV News

Mainte-nance of Both Cars

Caring for Kristen

Men's Club at Church

Scout Leader

Biking With Friend

Volunteer at Home-less Shelter

Weekends Away

Expand-ing the Family Room

Reprinted with permission from *Structured Exercises in Stress Management, Volume 1*, copyright 1983, 1994. Donald A. Tubesing. Published by Whole Person Associates Inc, 210 West Michigan, Duluth, MN 55802-1908, 218-727-0500.

Talk together about what you see happening in the daily life of Dan and Maria. Are you beginning to understand their marriage? Their lifestyle? Their frustrations? Notice the balls they have dropped. Remember that each marriage has different dynamics but similar challenges, when it comes to juggling day by day.

Now it's time for each of you to complete your own juggling-act diagram. Inside the balls in the air, write the various responsibilities, activities, and ongoing daily or weekly tasks you are trying to juggle. Inside the balls at the bottom of the diagram, write those things that you have had to drop along the way. Draw additional balls if you need them. Take your time.

_____'s Juggling Act
(her name)

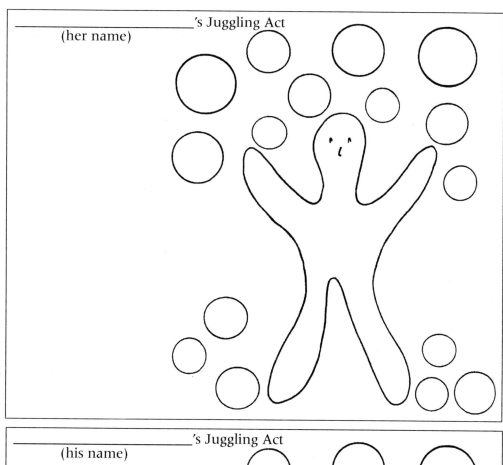

_____'s Juggling Act
(his name)

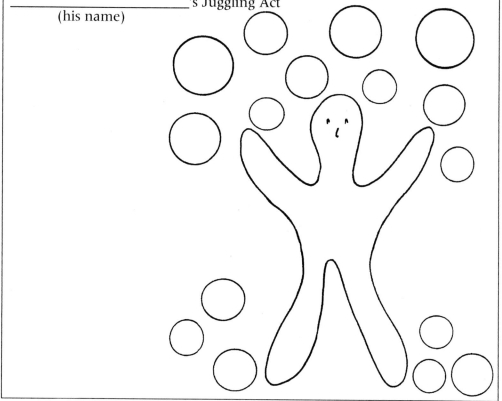

When both of you have finished, take a stretch break. Share a cold drink and perhaps a snack. Take a moment to thank God for giving you the things you really need in the midst of day-by-day challenges.

Move now to another location—outside, if weather permits—taking your juggling act diagrams with you. Take turns looking at each other's diagrams, without making any comment. Then share what you see as you look at them together. Think about this as taking a glimpse into the day-by-day feelings each of you has about the life you share—sort of like an X ray or MRI of what's going on inside you.

Now talk briefly about those things you and your spouse may have forgotten to include in your diagrams. Had you realized what you had dropped in your attempts to juggle everything? Remember that your questions and comments should be "open exploration," with each of you listening to the other, rather than being critical.

Perhaps you are one of the rare couples who discover that you haven't needed to drop anything, that your priorities are in order, and that your daily life is not rushed—no overload. If so, congratulations! You might want to add a few "balls" to your juggling act, if your life seems to need something more interesting or adventuresome! More than likely, however, you have found that your juggling act needs a little work! If you cannot continue now, plan a time when you can talk more about your day-by-day juggling and the stress that results from it.

2. Juggling and Stress

Devotional Thought: "Peace I leave with you; my peace I give to you" (John 14:27). Think about the ways in which you need a sense of peace at different times of the day.

Prayer: Thank you, God, for the peace you can give us as we juggle our busy lives. Help us to know what to drop and what to pick up. May we see all of life as an adventure and live each day and moment the best we can—alone, together, and with you. Amen.

Find a comfortable place where you can relax as you share together. Put your feet up, if you like. Read this section together quietly, as you relax, holding the book between you.

Are you feeling any stress or tension at this moment? Recognize this as a part of the cause and effect of overload in many marriages. More important than recognizing that often there is too much to manage on a daily basis is the recognition of the effect of this, which usually is not seen at first glance. *Stress* is the word most frequently used to define this effect.

You have looked at all the balls you are juggling day by day. Does this cause stress for you? Much has been written about stress. Studies show that people everywhere juggle many things that cause stress: jobs, family, and numerous activities. Even "good" or "happy" events and experiences can cause stress, such as a wedding or job promotion. Hans Slye, creator of the Stress Scale, defines this as "unstress," or happy stress. Most often, stress results when we try to juggle too much, especially if we become overloaded and tense.

Physicians tell us that juggling too many balls or doing too much in a tense, worried way may affect our immune system. As a result, we may be more likely to become sick, our blood pressure may be elevated, and we may experience heart attacks and other health problems.

On the other hand, some people are able to juggle many different things because of the way they relax their bodies and minds, determine their priorities, and say "no" when they have too much on their "platters." Most of all, these persons take control of their thoughts, with the help of God, to keep themselves "at peace" and to handle their lives creatively.

Pause now for a few minutes before continuing.

A Reflective Exercise

1. Can you recall persons whom you know—including sisters, brothers, family members, parents, other relatives, and friends—who may have juggled too much in the past or are now living in stressful, worried ways? Do you know anyone who has had a heart attack from stress and overwork?

   How do you think they juggled everything? In a positive or negative way? Talk about this now. Do not be judgmental of friends or family. This exercise is intended to help prevent *you* from doing too much in a negative way.

2. Ask each other: Is there more stress in our marriage than we have realized or admitted? When? Where? How do we handle it? How does stress relate directly or indirectly to the activities we are juggling? How does this compare to our priorities? (Allow time for each of you to respond.)

Where is our source of help?
"I lift up my eyes to the hills . . ."
Where does our help come from?
Our "help comes from the LORD, who made heaven and earth"
(Psalm 121:1-2).

God has given us ways to manage and cope with what we must do in each situation, relationship, conflict, and circumstance that comes along. We need to count on God's help.

Who is our best example? Jesus showed us how to handle juggling and stress. Many people made demands on him. They crowded around him to be healed. They gathered by the thousands to hear him preach. They pressed against him in crowds, like the woman who wanted simply to touch him. The disciples, the Pharisees, and others along the way asked many questions.

What did Jesus do? Being human as well as divine, his body became tired and needed sleep and relaxation—even in days considered less stressful than our age. Sometimes he took a boat to get away and relax from the pressures. One time, we understand, he slept in the fishing boat during a storm. Talk about being relaxed! Could we do that?

Other days he went to the mountain to pray. He also went to homes for meals and enjoyed sharing with people there and at weddings.

Most of all, in spite of a tired body, we know his mind was at peace no matter what he did, for he said, "Peace . . . Peace I leave with you. Let not your hearts be troubled." Jesus is our best example of how to handle the stress caused by daily pressures.

3. Juggling and Relaxing

Throughout this chapter the focus has been on what happens day by day within your circle of love, your marriage. Each marriage has a different scenario, yet *all* marriages are affected, either positively or negatively, by daily patterns of activity. Each partner in a marriage relaxes in different ways, which help to alleviate the stress of the daily "juggling act."

Relaxation Checklist

As each of you glance at the activities listed below, make a mental note of what you find most relaxing as an individual or as a couple.

__ reading	__ playing golf	__ aerobics
__ playing with children	__ relaxation exercises	__ being out in nature
__ swimming	__ listening to music	__ yoga
__ walking	__ talking with friends	__ computer games
__ watching TV	__ making love	__ dancing
__ other		

Now share with each other what you selected as most relaxing. Talk about which of these you want to do more often, alone and together. Then check these with a pencil or pen.

As individuals and as couples, it is essential to learn how to juggle, how much to juggle, and how to relax. The key is how to do this day by day! Again, Jesus showed us how. Here are some ways you can deal with the stress of "juggling."

---

10 Ways to Handle Stress

1. Try to relax while working, driving, or doing any activity, keeping alert at the same time. Check to see if your arms and legs are tense. Con-

---

Do-It-Yourself Marriage Enrichment

sciously relax them. Breathe deeply and say, "I am at peace," or "Lord, be with me today," as you prepare for some activity.

2. Take time to "smell the flowers." Delight in the ocean or a sunset, and really know what it is to be alive.

3. Laugh *at yourself* and *with others*. Enjoy humor without hurtful teasing.

4. Don't fret the small stuff! Ask yourself, "In all eternity, what will this matter?"

5. Try to be realistic about time commitments, allowing more time for each activity rather than crowding too much in a day.

6. Try not to be "anxious" or worry. Use your thought process to decide, "I am going to enjoy this day. I will be relaxed, knowing that God is always with me in whatever I am doing—in the little things as well as in the most important ones."

7. Try to start each day with God, using a devotional reading together or separately. "Wait on the Lord." "Be still." "Lift your eyes unto the hills" (the sky, the clouds). Possibly start writing your "thought-feelings" for a few minutes, and then leave any concerns with God. Here's what Maria might write:

   Dear God, thank you for this day. I have so much going on and I'm not sure I can get it all done. I am worried about Kristen being sick and about my meeting today. Be with my mother who is so alone after Dad died. Help me, Lord, to be at peace about everything. Amen.

8. Be at peace at the end of the day, forgiving each other and other people. Lay aside guilt. Place all concerns with God. Hold hands together and say a simple prayer before getting in bed, such as: "Thank you, Lord, for this day, for our lives together, and for your love and ours."

9. Deal with juggling and stress creatively. Try different methods.

10. Accept yourself as God's creation.

Take time now to think and talk together about how you can use these ways to deal with stress.

4. Juggling and Scheduling

Let's tune in again to Dan and Maria, as they are looking at each other's juggling act. Read their conversation aloud, imagining how they might be talking to each other. Put yourselves into it!

Dan: Look at all those "heavy" balls you are juggling! Are you trying to make me feel guilty? I *do* help with some of the grocery shopping and with keeping the house neat!

Maria: Why didn't you put those on your sheet too?

Dan: Well, I thought those things were mostly your role, and besides, I had used up all my balls.

Maria: Aren't they also your role? You could add some more balls!

Dan: Maybe I will, but there's only so much I can do! Right now I'm making supper on the nights you're in class, and I always make breakfast and our lunches.

Maria: Good for you! But you *did* forget my lunch last week, the day you had that noon meeting at a restaurant downtown. Besides, you don't make breakfast all the time, and you can hardly call toast and coffee "breakfast" on those mornings you leave early!

Dan: Okay, but I was a little stressed out last week. I'm not trying to prove anything. I just don't like being so overwhelmed most of the time, trying to get Kristen to day care and continually worrying about being late. At the same time, I wish I could pick up some of the things I've dropped.

Maria: I know, Dan; I feel the same way. Maybe it will be better after next semester. Why don't we see if there is something we can do about it even now? I'm sorry if I was critical. Let's take a look at our Saturdays. We don't have to juggle all the extra things on one day.

Dan: How about dropping some of these balls and picking up others? Or maybe we could just drop everything for a while!

Maria: Great idea! But it's impossible, Dan!

Dan: I know, but we've got to do *something!*

How were Dan and Maria talking together? Were they really listening to each other? Understanding? Sometimes critical? Share together now.

In their conversation that Sunday night, Dan and Maria began to focus on a plan. The word *flexible* seemed to be the key. As they explored their daily schedules, the "what if" question surfaced continually. They asked themselves, "What if we changed this or that, in our scheduling related to Kristen, meal times, and all the other things we have to do?"

One thing that seemed to be missing was some time to connect their lives with God. They wondered, "What if we could start each day by focusing for ten minutes together on a brief devotion to center our lives on God and remind us that God is with us throughout the day?" It sounded impossible at first, but as they developed their calendar, listing all the hours in the day and everything they were attempting to juggle, they decided to try to get up a little earlier each morning.

Dan and Maria also agreed to share some of the responsibilities more creatively. They further decided to take time each Sunday night to evaluate the past week and update specific roles and events for the coming week. They agreed that flexibility would need to be the theme of ongoing review and revisions in the scheduling process.

Take time now to look carefully at your own weekly schedule and talk about it together. Use the following calendar to do an overview of your week-ly schedule, including those responsibilities you listed in your individual Jug-gling Act diagrams. Then discuss what revisions are needed. (Note: You will need to make several copies of the blank calendar to use for your revisions.) This process will take some careful sharing and the willingness to listen to each other's ideas and suggested changes. At first the exercise may seem tedious, but it will begin to pay off in ways you might not imagine. When you are satisfied with your schedule, put a copy on your refrigerator door and copy it in your personal calendars and/or one you may keep together.

Our Weekly Schedule

TIME	MONDAY	TUESDAY	WEDNESDAY	THURSDAY	FRIDAY	SATURDAY	SUNDAY
5:00 A.M.							
6:00 A.M.							
7:00 A.M.							
8:00 A.M.							
9:00 A.M.							
10:00 A.M.							
11:00 A.M.							
12:00 P.M.							
1:00 P.M.							
2:00 P.M.							
3:00 P.M.							
4:00 P.M.							
5:00 P.M.							
6:00 P.M.							
7:00 P.M.							
8:00 P.M.							
9:00 P.M.							
10:00 P.M.							
11:00 P.M.							

Now look together at this five-point plan for dealing with stress.

Five Things We Will Try to Do as We Juggle Day by Day

1. We recognize that most people must juggle many things each day and week. It is part of life.
2. We acknowledge the link between our attitudes about things we have to do and our body's stress-producing systems.
3. We will freely admit any difficulties we have and talk about them in a noncritical way.
4. We will try to set aside time each morning for a brief devotion, so that Christ can guide us as we begin each day.
5. We will be sensitive to what we say to each other and to others, so that we do not cause extra stress for ourselves and others.

Can you, as marriage partners, affirm these steps as a part of your plan for the future? Talk about what is really involved in such a five-point outlook. Then take a few minutes to ask God's blessing and guidance on the ways you spend your time day by day.

Time management requires perspective beyond oneself. The writer of Ecclesiastes, known as "the preacher," expressed it this way: "[There is] a time for every matter under heaven" (3:1). It is this sense of time that is important, as God's time and your time become synchronized toward the greatest good within each day.

Howard Thurman has written about this need. Share this prayer of his as you read aloud together.

> I need Thy Sense of Order
> The confusion of the details of living
> Is sometimes overwhelming. The little things
> Keep getting in my way providing ready-made
> Excuses for failure to do and be
> What I know I ought to do and be.
> Much time is spent on things that are not very important,
> While significant things are put into an insignificant place.
> In my scheme of order I must unscramble my affairs
> So that my life will become order. O God, I need
> thy sense of order.
> From *Deep Is the Hunger* by Howard Thurman

Now conclude this time together by joining hands and saying to each other: "I thank God for you and the time we can share."

3. LET'S TALK IT OVER

▼

As you begin this chapter
▲ Play some of your favorite music.
▲ Find something each of you gave the other, either before or after you were married—something that has special meaning for you. It could be a shell your husband found at the beach or a special card from your wife, a pressed flower, a gift—something either romantic or humorous. Be imaginative.
▲ Find a comfortable place, take a deep breath or two, relax, hug, and say to each other, "I love you." Then share your special object. Don't hurry. You are setting the mood.

1. How's Our Communication?

> **Devotional Thought:** "Abraham...laughed ...Sarah laughed" (Genesis 17:17; 18:12); "A cheerful heart is a good medicine" (Proverbs 17:22).
>
> What makes *you* laugh? It has been said that laughter is the glue of love. Do you see humor in situations? Laugh *with* each other? Take lightly everyday frustrations or small things that happen?
>
> **Prayer:** Dear God, thank you for the ability to laugh and not take ourselves too seriously. We know you must have a good laugh when you hear some of our conversations. Thank you for this time together. Amen.

Talk together about a funny experience or situation that perhaps only the two of you know about. Try to hold on to this feeling and really enjoy each other as you make your way through this chapter, openly exploring how you talk together.

Begin by imagining how you would like to greet each other at the end of the day. You are tired. Maybe the baby cried most of the day, or your work situations were especially difficult, or one of you had a good day while the other had a bad day. How would you like your partner to greet you? Lovingly? Attentively? Quietly? To help you make these feelings clear to each other, each of you complete the following sentence:

When we greet each other at the end of a busy day and I am super tired,

I would like to _____ and

would like you to _____.

Now meet Jeff and Diane, who are in their first year of marriage. Both are mature and successful, with well-established careers and a future that seems most promising.

Their wedding day was celebrated by family members and friends who all agreed their marriage was ideal. They had a lovely wedding, with just a few glitches. Diane's mother walked out of her shoe as she went down the aisle, and Celeste, one of Diane's bridesmaids, almost fainted at the altar. Afterward, everyone laughed about these events.

By now Jeff and Diane have established priorities, managed to juggle many activities, and seem to be thriving. Yet their communication as husband and wife, which has slipped since they were first married, is the one area that needs growth.

Tune in on an average weekday, late afternoon. Diane has arrived home from work first, as usual, and is sitting at the kitchen table, looking at the mail and separating bills from correspondence, when Jeff walks in.

Jeff: Hi, honey! How was your day? *(He reaches for Diane and they hug briefly.)*

Diane: *(Opening another envelope, barely looking up)* The same as always. How was yours? I have some cookies and iced tea for you.

Jeff: Love your chocolate-chip cookies! How did you have time to make these after work? *(Taking a bite)* Mmm.... How was my day? Nothing new. *(He grabs another cookie and takes off his jacket and tie while he reaches in the closet for his golf shoes.)* I'm going over to the driving range to meet Bill. We're getting ready for the tournament Saturday.

Diane: Why didn't you tell me you were going to the driving range tonight? I planned an early dinner, and I wanted to . . . "

Jeff: What's the big deal? It's only 5:30, and I *did* tell you, Diane. I mentioned it to you right after I got off the phone with Bill last night. I think *you* were reading the paper.

Diane: No, you never told me, Jeff. I would remember. You *never* tell me your plans ahead of time!

Jeff: *You* just weren't listening. You *never* listen.

Diane: That's not fair, Jeff. I *do* listen, but you don't take time to explain things. I never heard you say anything about meeting Bill tonight. That will take an hour and a half.

Jeff: So? We can eat when I get back.

Diane: I had wanted us to eat so we could go to the early movie—that one we talked about. It's the last night for it.

Jeff: You never told me.

Diane: Yes, I did, Jeff—this morning over coffee—and you said, "Okay" and kept on reading the paper. You weren't listening.

Jeff: *(Almost yelling)* It's my only chance to read the newspaper. Besides, this is a stupid conversation. I promised Bill I'd meet him at 5:45, and I'm keeping my word! I'll be back around 7:00. *(Jeff walks out, slamming the door. Diane, still sitting at the table, is almost in tears. She breaks in half a pencil she has been holding.)*

Talk together a few minutes about what was helpful and unhelpful about the greeting and conversation of Diane and Jeff.

Helpful	*Unhelpful*
Hugging when they saw each other	Using the word *never*
Having cookies ready for Jeff	Interrupting each other
Complimenting Diane's cookies	Criticizing and accusing each other
Other:	Other:

How could they have changed their communication? Share your ideas now for a few minutes.

Communication sometimes breaks apart, like a pencil under force; and sometimes it is cut off with the crashing of a slammed door. Why does this happen? How can it be prevented?

Through all the years—not just while dating or during the honeymoon phase—we need to be open-hearted, loving, and caring—cherishing the one we have promised to love. This is our primary circle—the circle of love.

At this time you might like to take a break—go for a walk, get a snack, stretch or exercise for a few minutes. Allow five or ten minutes, then come back together.

2. The Open Line

Devotional Thought: "There was silence in heaven for about half an hour" (Revelation 8:1); "Be still, and know that I am God" (Psalm 46:10).

Is there ever a time for silence between husband and wife? A time to listen to what the other person is saying and feeling? A time when angry or hurtful words are rethought into caring statements or nonattacking words? Yes! Silent listening is an essential part of communication.

Prayer: (Pause for a brief moment of silence.) Lord, guide our sharing, thinking, and talking together now, we pray. Amen.

If you have a cordless or cellular telephone, get it at this time to remind you of your communication as a couple. The telephone, one of the best means of communication, symbolically represents how we can relate to problems and find solutions through communication. Ideally, the "line" should always be "open" between husband and wife. But that's not always how it is in the real world. *Communication*—a word, a process—is the key to understanding. Perhaps more has been written about communication than about any other aspect of relationships or responsibilities—whether in business, organizations, politics, technology, or marriage. Yet what we know about communication is meaningless unless we put it into practice.

Sometimes those who are intimate with each other and have been together for years take their relationship for granted and become less thoughtful with their words than when speaking to a friend or coworker. Shouldn't our best friend be the one to whom we are married? Psychologists tell us the main reason that lasting marriages endure is because the husband and wife consider themselves best friends. When we treat our loved one, our partner, as a *friend,* we place a high value on communication.

Much in the wife-husband relationship depends, to a great extent, on the ability to communicate effectively. With effective communication, many concerns in a marriage can be worked out. Yet communication involves many variables: feelings, fears, memories, hopes, and the complexity of daily life. Communication requires effort and time.

When we say to each other, "Let's talk it over," we are opening the door to understanding; yet too often we neglect this kind of open sharing because we think we don't have time. Most married couples need to give more attention to sharing, listening, and hearing what each person is seeking to express. The question is, *How do we keep the line open?*

Keeping the Line Open

Having your "line" open to your partner is essential to effective communication. What are some ways to do this?

Be Aware of How Our Parents Talked to Each Other

This is a very important factor in every marriage. Often these role models or examples are the ones we consciously—or more frequently, unconsciously—follow in our own marriages. Sometimes we don't want to continue in the ways our parents communicated.

Each of you share your responses to the following questions about how your parents related in your childhood home. If you came from a single-parent family, consider what patterns of communication were evident.

1. Did each parent allow the other to talk? Did they really listen to each other?
2. How did your parent(s) listen to you when you were a child? When you were hurt? How did your parent(s) react when you cried? When

you did something wrong, how were you disciplined? Did your parent(s) "yell" when angry or withdraw?

3. Do you see any repeating patterns that are helpful or unhelpful in your marriage? Each of you examine yourself in this regard.

Now complete these statements to yourself. Then share together.

Sometimes I think I communicate as my mother/father did in a helpful way, such as _____; in an unhelpful way, such as _____.

Listen to each other without agreeing or disagreeing, letting your partner share her/his insights. Identify any repeating patterns of your parents that you might like to change.

Feeling Good About Ourselves.

If we feel good about ourselves, we are more apt to listen—to "have our hearts open"—to other people and to our partner, hearing and understanding the pain, frustrations, concerns, and feelings.

Because we are God's creations, not "junk," it is important that we "love our neighbor *as ourself.*" God intends us to love *ourself* as well as our neighbor, which often we misunderstand. Jesus meant for us to fully love others and respect ourselves, too.

Unfortunately, many people do not really like themselves. We can nurture, encourage, listen, and help build up our mates; however, if for some reason a spouse's self-esteem has been badly damaged in the past, he or she may need to seek counseling or professional help. Even so, the words we say to our loved ones can help or hurt. You will want to think carefully about your self-esteem and talk about how you can help each other in this area. Remember that even if you have strong self-esteem, it is important to build up and encourage each other daily.

Keeping in Touch.

Perhaps the most important way to maintain good communication is to take the time to talk to each other each day, just as you do with friends and coworkers. Ask yourselves: Do we find time to talk together each day? Does each of us allow the other to share his or her feelings? If there is too much to cover at a certain time, do we set another date for talking more about these concerns? Because "keeping in touch" each day and deciding when you have time to talk together about important matters and concerns are so important to your marriage, let's explore this in more detail.

On the Line Together

There's no doubt about it: We need to be intentional about setting apart some time when we can be "on the line" together, yet this is not always easy because of complex schedules, children, interruptions, and time pressures. To combat this problem, some couples "check in" with each other during the day by phone, if they have the time and freedom, to share a little about what is happening and "take the edge off" some of the day's frustrations before arriving home. Other couples leave notes for each other in lunches, briefcases, or other places where they are sure to be found during the day.

Perhaps one of the most crucial times to be "on the line" with your spouse is when you greet each other after being apart for most of the day. As Jeff and Diane showed us earlier, the way we communicate in these few minutes sets the tone for the rest of the evening—and can contribute to longer-lasting positive or negative feelings about our relationship.

Jean was on the phone with her best friend, Sue, when Ted walked in the door after work. Putting down his things, he waited for a moment for her to end the conversation, but she continued to talk about what he considered a trivial matter—Sue's vacation plans for the summer. Growing more and more impatient, he told Jean that he wanted to talk to her. Annoyed by the interruption, she held her finger to her mouth, trying to shush him, and motioned for him to leave.

Ted walked away feeling very upset. He had wanted to talk to Jean about some relationship problems he was having at work, realizing that she relates better to people than he does. At that moment, it seemed to him that she didn't care as much about him as she did about Sue.

How could Jean and Ted have handled the situation better? What would you do in a similar situation?

One idea you might try is to agree not to take phone calls during the time you expect to be reunited at the end of the day. Or if one of you is talking on the phone when the other returns, tell the person on the other end of the line that you will call back later. Then spend a few minutes greeting each other and talking about the day. In some instances, one or both partners may need some time and space before sharing or discussing anything.

Some couples find it helpful to have a snack to take the edge off their hunger and then sit down and talk briefly before getting ready for the evening meal, reserving more leisurely conversation for dinnertime or later. These couples know that it's unwise to talk about important concerns or issues when you are hungry. It's also good to avoid having serious conversations at bedtime, when you are tired. Such times are potentially a setup for frustration or a never-ending discussion. If your evening schedule is tight with commitments, save major discussions for another time.

Whenever you find time to talk together, remember that the television and newspaper are distractions and can keep you from communicating effectively. Background music, however, can create a mood and help you relax, leading to a productive time of sharing. The key is giving each other your full attention.

When Do You Talk?

When do you have a chance to really talk together—not just about the weather and details of daily living, but about your feelings? Ask yourselves these questions:

1. When do we truly share our feelings with each other each day?
   _____ At the beginning of the day or at breakfast
   _____ Phone calls during the day
   _____ Lunch together or evening meals
   _____ In the evening after eating or before going to bed
   _____ Other times: _____

2. When do we have more time to talk during the week? _____
   on weekends?
   _____ Friday night   _____ Saturday during the day
   _____ Saturday night
   _____ "on a date" _____ Sunday _____ Other times: _____

3. Do we have enough time to talk on a deeper level, setting aside routine concerns and focusing on what we need to share from the heart?

Let's tune in again to Jeff and Diane. It's the morning after the night the door was slammed and the pencil was broken. Read their conversation aloud, taking their roles. Put yourselves into it!

Jeff: I'm really sorry about last night. I guess I don't tell you enough about what I plan to do, and I realize I'm not always listening.

Diane: I'm sorry, too, Jeff, and I know that cold dinner last night wasn't very good. We didn't get to see the movie, but maybe we can rent the video sometime.

Jeff: I tried to "make up," but nothing seemed to work. I guess I wasn't trying in the right way.

Diane: Well, by then I did have a headache. It wasn't a good time to make up like you wanted to. Besides, I usually like to talk about my feelings before we make love.

Jeff: I know. Maybe we need some help learning how to talk to each other. We're each on our own wavelength. We think we're sharing ideas, but we aren't getting through. It's like a bad phone connection—like static on the line.

Diane: What can we do about it?

Jeff: Well, here's one idea. I have an opportunity to go to a seminar on communication sponsored by my company. It's at a downtown hotel two weeks from now. I could get continuing education credit. It wouldn't cost anything, and you probably could join me as a spouse. What do you think?

Diane: Would that really help us? I know some of the ideas would apply to business *and* marriage, but marriage is a little different. Besides, I think we need to invest something of ourselves—our free time and whatever it costs—so that it's just for *us*. My sister and her husband went to a marriage retreat one weekend, and she said it helped them so much. I don't know how much it cost.

Jeff: Well, your sister and that strange husband of hers do need a lot of help. I don't think *we're* in crisis. Everybody says we're the ideal couple.

Diane: I wish you wouldn't be so judgmental about my sister's marriage! And I know that you don't want to spend extra money, although I'm sure we have enough for this kind of thing. No, we're not in crisis, but I think we could improve how we talk to each other. Let me get some information about a one-day marriage seminar. I'll even go to your company's training, if you want. I think I can get the day off.

Although it was not a complete solution and it was not really a compromise or negotiation, Diane and Jeff did attend the company-sponsored seminar and discovered some communication concepts that related to their marriage. Not only did they have a good time, but they also were able to evaluate *how* they talk to each other.

It is not necessary to go to a special seminar or retreat in order to improve your marriage. In fact, you are doing that *right now!*

After a short break, take some time to evaluate *how* you talk together.

3. How Do We Talk Together?

If possible, make a copy of the following exercise so that each of you may complete it separately. Otherwise, mark your responses in your notebooks.

How Am I Doing?

How do I talk to my spouse? To answer this question, make a mark on the lines to show how you see yourself now. Be honest with yourself.

LISTENING

I listen when you talk to me and wait until you have finished speaking. I do not think of what I am going to say next and try not to interrupt.

Seldom   Most of the time

_____

UNDERSTANDING

I try to understand and empathize, to see how *you* feel. I let you know I understand, even when I feel differently.

Seldom   Most of the time

OPENNESS

I express my thoughts, feelings, and wants freely and talk about them to let you know how I am honestly feeling within. I try not to come on "too strong" or be too demanding.

Seldom   Most of the time

WORDS I USE

I do not tease (if it is hurtful), "put you down," call you names, lecture, or withdraw. I try to be polite when we are with others. I try not to "prove my point" or be argumentative, even when I don't agree with what you have said.

Seldom   Most of the time

ACCEPTANCE

I accept you. I love you unconditionally, as God does, even when my point of view is different. I will try to change myself when I feel I am not right and hope you will do the same. But regardless of our differences, I accept you as a unique person and creation.

Seldom   Most of the time

FOCUSING ON "THE NOW"

I try to talk about "the now" and not bring up past conversations unless we have enough time to discuss and resolve previous concerns. I concentrate on the "here and now."

Seldom   Most of the time

ASSERTIVENESS

I do not suffer in silence but express my feelings without being angry or aggressive, being willing to negotiate when necessary, and I want you to do the same.

Seldom   Most of the time

_____

RESPECT

I respect you as a person, even when I do not agree with you, just as I respect coworkers, neighbors, and others in a polite and considerate way.

Seldom   Most of the time

_____

Now come back together and briefly talk about how you evaluated yourselves. Then say to each other individually, "I am going to try to listen more and to be more understanding and careful about how I talk to you."

4. Trouble on the Line

Have you ever had trouble hearing someone on the telephone? There may have been static on the line caused by a storm, or perhaps the connection was broken. Likewise, sometimes our line of communication in marriage has trouble temporarily, and we must be aware of what these interruptions may be.

As one example of "trouble on the line," the words spoken by one partner are heard differently by the other. Sometimes it is helpful to imagine how the words we say are really heard, especially when different opinions and feelings already exist.

Jeff and Diane tried to imagine how each one "received" a particular message from the other by using the diagram of a telephone. The examples they used were similar to conversations they had experienced earlier. Look together at the diagram of the phone conversation, found on the page following.

Do you recall a time when you may have said something that sounded quite clear to you but may have been heard somewhat differently by your spouse? What could have caused that difference? Was it the way you said it? Were emotions overriding words? Were there other factors that entered into the dynamics of the conversation?

What Jeff said:
"I'm sorry I can't go with you to the picnic with your relatives this weekend. I've got to be at the office finishing up that special project."

What Diane said:
"I'm really too tired to go with you and your friends to the golf tournament, and I hope you won't mind if I stay home and catch up on things here."

What Diane heard:
"I don't want to go with you to the picnic because my work is really more important—and you didn't come to my family reunion last year."

What Jeff heard:
"I don't like golf, and I think the whole thing is a waste of time. I really don't care what you think—just give some excuse for me not being there."

Jeff reflects on what he said—and on what Diane may have heard.

Diane reflects on what she said—and on what Jeff may have heard.

Is There "Trouble on the Line?"

Each of you take a few minutes to write in the telephone diagrams below something you might have said and what your partner might have heard. Adapt a previous conversation or write an imaginary one.

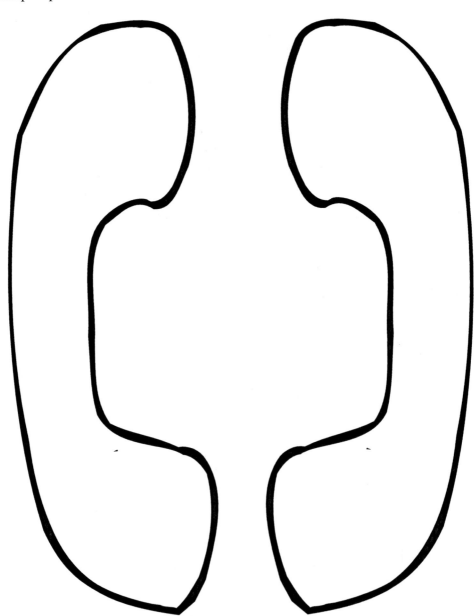

What you might have said and what your wife might have heard.

What you might have said and what your husband might have heard.

Without looking at each other's copy, read aloud to each other what you wrote. Discuss whether this was the way it really happened—or might happen. How could you avoid such "trouble" when communicating in the future?

The latest studies show that four behaviors related to communication are hurtful and can lead to the end of a marriage if repeated over a long time. They are *criticism, contempt, defensiveness,* and *withdrawal.* Howard Markman, psychology professor at the University of Denver, states that even when there is a considerable amount of empathy and understanding, these "zingers" or "negative behaviors" may erase the positive acts of kindness in a marriage.

Markmam illustrates that it is the wife who generally is more emotionally invested in the marriage and is the caretaker of the relationship. If the husband believes she is critical of him, he may withdraw instead of talking about her concerns and feelings. She then may criticize more. He may become more defensive and withdraw even more.

All this might lead to what we call the "hamster wheel cycle." Have you ever seen a hamster go around the little wheel, jump off, and then get back on, continuing the pattern of going nowhere and stopping every so often? This cycle of communication can continue endlessly.

As we've already seen, one of the greatest barriers to communication in the circle of love is to greet each other with critical words, such as, "Did you wear *that* tie/outfit to work?" or "Late again?" or "Why didn't you call?" Such words stifle the sharing of reasons or feelings. Any criticism such as, "You forgot the cleaning, didn't you?" or "You forgot to call me," spoken in an accusing tone, tends to prevent a loving conversation between a couple. Likewise, a long list of everything that went wrong during the day—"My boss complained about my work; everyone dumped their jobs on my desk; the 'carry in' that someone ordered was cold and tasteless; I'll never meet my deadline," or "Jimmy's sick; Betty failed math this term; Rich got in trouble with his teacher again"—can inhibit further communication. Talk a few minutes about these behaviors.

Now, answer the following questions quietly to yourselves and then talk about them together.

---

1. Do I try to give the answer or solution too quickly?
   _____ rarely _____ sometimes _____ often

Example #1   Sharon: I'm so tired because of all the papers I must grade each night.
             Doug: Why don't you just quit teaching!

Example #2   David: Your parents are driving me nuts.
             Karen: Just don't see them anymore.

The answers given in the above examples are quick, unrealistic "fix-it" answers. Simply listening or "mirroring" would be more helpful, such as, "It does sound as if you have to grade papers every night," or "My parents do bother you, don't they?"

2. Do I downplay my partner's feelings?
_____ rarely _____ sometimes _____ often

Example #1
Kevin: I had a terrible day at work. I feel awful.
Sharon: Everybody does sometimes. You'll feel better tomorrow.

Example #2   Barb is on a diet. On Saturday morning her husband brings home a dozen doughnuts, which she loves but has not bought for a while.

Barb: How *could* you, Bill? You know I'm trying to lose weight.
Bill: It's Saturday. Don't get mad and ruin our day!

In the first example, Sharon is discounting her husband's feelings rather than listening and understanding. A better response would be, "It does sound bad," or "You really are upset, aren't you, Kevin?" or "Tell me what happened."

In the second example, Bill discounted Barb's diet; then he downplayed her feelings. Instead, he might have said, "I'm sorry, Barb. I could freeze them and take them to the office next week."

Other communication blocks that cause trouble "on the line" are changing the subject; not using "I" statements, such as "*I feel bad when you . . .*" rather than "*You always make me feel bad*"; attacking the other person, walking out of the room during a discussion, without saying that you need a little time to think or that you would rather talk about it later; and turning away, ignoring, or withdrawing. Also, certain ways of saying things, such as, "You *never heard* of Sadat?" can imply that your partner is "stupid" for not knowing something. Comments such as "I'll do it on my terms" and "Why don't you . . . " and "Yes, but . . . " are other games couples frequently play as they go around in circles about projects or things that need to be done, causing trouble "on the line" of communication.

So, what can be done to repair trouble "on the line" and avoid any future problems? Take a short break if you need one and then begin to explore some of the ways you can improve your communication.

5. Repair Service

Jeff and Diane are really trying to improve their communication. They have arranged to meet after work at a nearby restaurant to make plans for a vacation. Jeff is sitting at a booth, waiting for Diane, who is running late. He is looking at his watch with the menu open on his placemat. Diane rushes into the restaurant, loaded with travel brochures. She slips into the booth looking somewhat anxious, realizing she has kept Jeff waiting.

Read their dialogue as you assume their roles. Put yourselves into their conversation.

Diane: I'm sorry I'm late. How long have you been here?

Jeff: Let's see . . . *(looking at watch)*, only one hour and six minutes.

Diane: You are being more patient than usual, then! *(smiling slightly)* I know it couldn't have been more than fifteen minutes, and I would have been on time if the travel agent hadn't taken phone calls while I was waiting for these *(motioning to travel folders)*.

Jeff: Hey, I'm not upset at all. I was kidding about the time. Let's take a look at the menu and then check out the brochures. Remember what that counselor said about trying to make decisions on an empty stomach—that we should communicate when we're *not* hungry.

Diane: Jeff, what would you say if I told you I've already decided we're going to a deserted island where there's no TV or telephone? I know it's hard to believe, but after I picked up the brochures, I got in the car and opened a letter that came in the mail. I thought it was only advertising, but inside was the announcement that we have won a free trip to this island somewhere in the Pacific. The only catch is that we will receive one-way tickets. Airline service is being discontinued the day we arrive!

Jeff: What's happened to you, Diane? You've changed. I've never seen you so funny! But if you were really serious, I'd say, "Let's go!"

Jeff and Diane order their meals, laughing a lot as they imagine what would happen on a vacation on a deserted island. Before leaving the restaurant, they make plans to spend a week at a reasonable condo at the ocean, the one where they spent their honeymoon almost a year ago. They leave a larger tip than usual for the waitress and spend the rest of the evening talking together at home—in bed.

How do you feel about Jeff and Diane's communication at the restaurant? What was decidedly different from their previous conversations? Was it believable that they could be as relaxed and carefree as they seemed to be? If so, what do you think made the difference? How would *you* have interacted with each other in a similar situation? Discuss these questions.

How Can We Keep Our Line in Good Repair?

There are two major steps you can take to improve your communication.

1. Develop Conversational Intimacy.

After a couple marries, sometimes the emotional intimacy they have in conversation diminishes because of their busyness. Emotional intimacy must be developed continually.

Basically, there are three levels of communication:

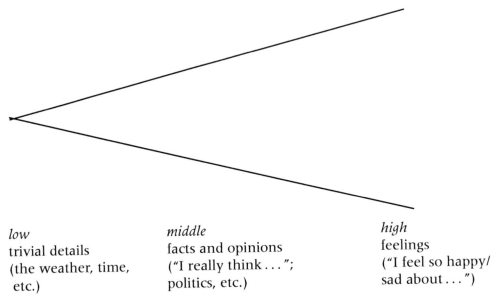

low
trivial details
(the weather, time,
   etc.)

middle
facts and opinions
("I really think...";
politics, etc.)

high
feelings
("I feel so happy/
sad about...")

It is natural for couples to talk about the day's plans, politics, the news, and opinions about different subjects. This kind of communication is often easier and safer than admitting weaknesses or feelings. It is very important, however, that a couple also continually communicate on the *feeling level*.

Much has been written about the different ways men and women communicate. Generally speaking, it is true that, in our culture, men have been encouraged to share their opinions and thoughts more than their feelings, whereas women have been encouraged to share their feelings. However, men can learn to share their feelings also.

What happens to a couple's marriage when neither partner communicates on the feeling level? If both communicate about facts and superficial subjects only, they will be unable to establish emotional intimacy, and as a result, they will distance themselves from each other. For example, a woman may talk about feeling sad because she and her husband have moved far away from her parents and friends. Her husband may listen briefly or "tune her out," or even say, "You said it once. Do you have to keep talking about it?" Actually, she does, for she is grieving, and talking helps the healing process.

On the other hand, a wife might notice her husband is very quiet, keeping his feelings to himself—perhaps as "taught" in his childhood home with words such as "be brave" or superficial conversation between his parents. So when his wife says, "Is something wrong?" he may respond, "Nothing," keeping frustrations about work or their marriage to himself. These feelings then may accumulate through the months and years, resulting in occasional inappropriate displays of anger or increasing withdrawal.

Many men—as well as some women—have been so carefully "taught" not to share their feelings that it takes a long time for them to recognize or identify their feelings of sadness or anger. Frequently they even believe it is *wrong* to say how they feel. They are often surprised to find that it is okay to have feelings and to express them. Of course, they must learn to express these feelings in the right way, without becoming upset or angry.

As we've said previously, using "I" statements is an effective way for both men and women to talk on the feeling level. Rather than saying "*You* make me feel so bad" or "*You* make me angry," for example, one might say, "*I* would be so happy if you would arrange it so that, instead of working, we can go out Friday night"; "*I* am really upset when you are late at night and don't call me"; "*I* feel bad when you joke about my weight"; or "*I* am upset when you criticize me."

Couples who never have used "I" statements often say something such as, "This is artificial. It's so hard to do." It *is* difficult to learn this method of expressing feelings, especially when one or both partners did not communicate in this way as a child. Generally it takes time to learn to communicate on the feeling level. Don't become discouraged if you forget or make mistakes; just keep trying. The key is to be intentional about it.

How can couples be intentional about communicating on the feeling level? If the husband is the one who is not sharing feelings, he must say to himself and to his wife, "It's all right to have these feelings and to share them with the one who loves and understands me, and I will try to remember to do this rather than withdraw or keep everything inside, building layers of anger or resentment." The wife, then, must be very careful to listen and not be judgmental about her husband's feelings, avoiding unhelpful comments such as, "I don't know why you feel that way. You shouldn't."

Likewise, the husband must listen to his wife when she shares her feelings, putting his arm around her and holding her tenderly. If she is angry, he may need to listen for a while before reaching out for her, so that she does not feel that he is trying to "fix it" by being sexually intimate. Again, saying things such as "It will be all right" and "You mustn't feel that way" and giving quick answers or advice such as, "Just go in and tell your boss or coworker what you think!" are not helpful responses. Most of all, he needs to listen caringly. Remember, the one who is sharing his or her feelings usually does not want advice or lectures but someone who will listen and understand.

Later on, after the one who has talked about his or her feelings for a while—perhaps even several times, depending on the degree or extent of sadness, grief, or anger—the "listener" may offer some ideas or suggestions about what might be helpful in a particular situation. Even then, however, the words spoken are extremely important. One might say, for example, "What about the possibility of doing this or that?" or "What ideas or options do you/we have to change this situation?" rather than, "You should do this."

We cannot overemphasize the importance of learning to share feelings. If you and your spouse do not grow in this way, it may be difficult for you to establish caring communication. Learning to talk on a feeling level will help you face both the smallest and most difficult situations in life, keep the lines of communication open, and enrich your circle of love. This leads to the second major step you can take to improve your communication.

2. Avoid Generalizations and Comparisons.

Certain words such as *never* and *always* can be accusatory. "You *never* talk to me"; "You *never* understand me"; "You *always* leave a mess around the house." Instead, say something such as, "I really like it when you talk to me," or "I need you to talk to me," or "I would really appreciate it if you could help more to keep the house clean."

Likewise, comparisons such as "Why are you like your father?" "Why can't you be like your friend Sharon? She cooks every night for Jim." "Skip does a great job on his lawn; why can't you?" "Couldn't you wear clothes like Marybeth?" are unhelpful and often diminish self-esteem.

Another frequent pattern of criticism is expressed in the words "You should have . . ." or "shouldn't have . . . ." This becomes a habit of "shoulds" or "shouldn'ts," which create negative feelings and responses.

In addition to these two major steps, there are other ways you can "keep the line open" as well as repair it when needed. Review the plan outlined below to see if you both agree that this can be your "communication commitment" for the future.

Our Plan for Keeping the Line Open

1. We will set aside some time each day, preferably after a meal or after children and others are cared for, to simply talk together about what's happening "inside us"—feelings, frustrations, dreams—as well as decisions that need to be made.
2. We will respect each other and truly "listen" without interrupting or finishing sentences of the other.
3. We will not use language that is explosive or embarrassing, or that in any way "puts down" the responses or feelings of the other. We will not yell at each other, even when we disagree.
4. We will be careful to "clarify" in the midst of our talking together so as not to confuse or leave out important details.
5. We will be "totally present" in conversations, patiently focusing on what is being said, rather than "jumping ahead" in our thoughts to other concerns.
6. We will be loving and forgiving at all times in our communication.

Signed _____
(wife)

_____
(husband)

Do We Need Operator Assistance?

When using the telephone, all of us occasionally need to press "0" for operator assistance as we seek to get additional information, make connections with someone who is hard to reach, or report trouble on the line. Likewise, in our marriages we also have the need for "operator assistance" when we cannot connect with each other as we want and need to do.

There are many sources of help, as we've indicated, but the greatest assistance comes from God; and the line of prayer is continually open. Always keep this in mind. Be ready to seek help, as the prophet reminds us: "Seek the LORD while he may be found, call upon him while he is near" (Isaiah 55:6).

Calling God is as easy as pressing a redial button on your telephone pad. There is never a busy signal on the line. Talk to God together now as you share in this brief conversation, alternating your voices.

Voice 1: Hello, God. This is _____ and _____. We just wanted to be in touch with you for a moment.

Voice 2: Yes, God, we know we need to talk with you and ask for direction and perspective as we work on our marriage. We especially want to ask you to let us know when we need to make some changes and try some new ways of talking together.

Voice 1: Could you tell us how we're doing right now—as you see us, as you know us?

Voice 2: (Answering the question as if God is speaking) "You two are on the way. Just keep open to each other, talk together about how you really feel, and listen well. Let love be in the words you speak. And remember, I'm here for you. I love you. Good-bye for now."

Together: Good-bye.

Close your time together with this simple prayer:

Dear God, help us always to be open to each other and open to you. Thank you for listening to us. Help us to listen to you. Amen.

4. ENERGIZING OUR MARRIAGE

▼

Before you begin this chapter

▲ take a short walk together, do a few exercises alone or together, look at something that energizes your lives together, such as flowers growing outside or a picture, listen to a lively piece of music, or sit quietly for a short time as you relax. Any of these ideas can help to revitalize you as individuals and as a couple. Many couples realize this, but no longer take time to do these things.

As you begin reading

▲ sit near a cozy lamp—or a warm fireplace, if it is cold outside—to symbolize energizing your marriage. If it is an especially hot day or evening, you might put a lightbulb or a battery beside you to signify energizing or recharging your marriage! *Always try to make this marriage enrichment workshop fun and creative. Use your ideas, too, to set the tone.*

Devotional Thought: "This is the day that the Lord has made; let us rejoice and be glad in it" (Psalm 118:24); "Do not worry about tomorrow" (Matthew 6:34).

As you begin each day, think about being happy. It may be more difficult for you to be cheerful in the morning if you are a "night person," but psychologists say that cognitively saying or thinking in your mind, "This day is going to be good" will help you to have a positive outlook. With God's help, it is even more probable that you will be glad—whatever each day you share together may bring.

Prayer: God, be with us now as we think and plan how we can keep our marriage energized.

It was a cold day. The wind was blowing, the grass had not yet turned green, and the first spring bulbs had just barely poked their stems out of the earth to test the weather. Inside, Betty and Jason, who had been married for almost two years, did not feel as much warmth in their marriage as they did in the comfortable heat of their small but attractive apartment. Their marriage could not be considered cold, or even chilly, but they definitely did not have the warming energy that comes from talking about everything, laughing while playing a game, relishing even the simplest fast-food meal, or feeling the closeness of their early days together—which they had thought would last forever.

Several months after the honeymoon, the energy they had given to their relationship had dwindled. Why not? They were married now, and there were "more important" things to do, they reasoned, such as "getting ahead" in their jobs, entertaining friends who had been neglected while they were more focused on each other, and working toward their goals of a bigger home and a new car. It was time to put their energy into other parts of their lives, right? Besides, if it didn't work out, they thought in the back of their minds, they always could get a divorce.

Does this scenario happen frequently? Unfortunately, the answer is yes. After the wedding, couples often "work" on other parts of their lives, putting less energy into their relationship. Knowing that divorce is so common now, some couples do not even try very hard to make their marriage work.

When you exchanged vows, the word *divorce* was not a part of them. Plan, therefore, to make your marriage last "as long as you both shall live," in whatever situations you find yourselves. This is the most important investment you can make in your lives—for you and your children.

Is your marriage full of energy? Wonderful! This chapter will give you lots of ideas about how to keep that energy flowing. If your marriage needs more energy, now is the time to think about it.

1. A Little Effort Can Produce a Lot of Energy

Let's "listen in" to a conversation between Betty and Jason. It's Sunday evening. The weekend has been very full, and many things have been left undone, such as paying bills, returning telephone calls, and doing the laundry. They cleaned the apartment on Saturday and spent all Sunday afternoon with Betty's parents, who live sixty miles away and insist on a visit at least once a month. They are now driving home. Assume their roles as you read their dialogue aloud. Put yourselves into their feelings, even though they might be quite different from your own.

Betty: I'm really worried about my mother. She seemed so tired today. She's got high blood pressure, she doesn't watch her diet, and she won't go to the doctor as often as she should.

Jason: I'm concerned about *you*, Betty. You seem pretty stressed out. Maybe you're like your mother, trying to do too much. That doesn't leave much time for us. It seems like we're always working on something!

Betty: That's just the way it is now, ever since we got married and set all those goals to get the things we wanted. We've had to work hard to make the money we need to pay the bills and the college loans, and the savings plan we set up is almost more than we can manage. Maybe we should have set five years rather than three years as the time when we would have enough for a down payment on a house.

Jason: Well, then, what about kids? Are we going to postpone them forever?

Betty: Jason, don't get me upset about having children! I do want to have children, but I want us to have a nice house first, with a nursery for the baby and some of the other things we need, so I won't have to work full time after the baby comes.

Jason: Speaking of working full time, it seems that our whole marriage is suffering because we do all the work that needs to be done, plus volunteering some, but we don't have any time to work on what's happening in *our lives*.

Betty: *You* should talk! I know we need the money, but with you working that second job, there's no time left for us.

Jason: Well, what do you want me to do—quit the job and let our charge card build up, like *you* let happen before?

Betty: It wasn't all my fault, Jason! You bought a lot of things on plastic, too! I wish there was another way, so that you wouldn't have to work at the video store four nights a week. I'm not too crazy about that kind of job anyway.

Jason: Part of our problem is managing the time we do have—like having to go visit your parents once a month. We spend a lot more time with your family than mine!

Betty: You family's two hundred miles farther away than mine! What do you expect?

Jason: Let's not get into an argument about our families! We've done enough of that before. I do think though, that we stay longer than we need to on these visits. Tonight I wish we could have left an hour earlier so we'd have some time for ourselves when we get home.

Betty: I know, Jason. I'm tired, too, but Dad really wanted to show us his slides of their trip out west, and I didn't want to disappoint him.

Jason: That's part of the trouble. You never want to disappoint your parents, but you don't seem to care if you disappoint *me!*

Betty: I never want to disappoint you, Jason. Maybe I just want everybody to be happy. It's a matter of priorities, I guess. Besides wanting everyone to be happy, I want some nice things for our home. That would make me happy.

Jason: What about me? I would like to be able to have this car worked on. It needs some major repairs. That would make *me* happy.

Betty: If you were more of a mechanic, like my brother, you'd be able to fix your car yourself.

Jason: Oh, come on now, Betty, I can't do everything! I do the best I can. I put in all those extra hours at the video store after my regular job, and I'm beat by the end of the day! You've got a lot easier job working at the beauty salon.

Betty: Are you kidding? I stand on my feet all day and take care of those people who come in each week, telling me all their problems and wanting to look like a movie star when they leave! Not many look like that. And I have to try to be so pleasant, even when I don't feel like it, that I don't even want to talk when I come home at the end of the day. Besides, when I do come home, you're not there most of the time! I really want to get my degree finished at the college, too. I don't mind doing this for now, but I don't want to do it forever.

Jason: Well, at least I bring home a lot of free videos, and you can watch those when I'm not there.

Betty: Well, that's true. At least I have a chance to relax once in a while, and I do appreciate that. It's just that I think we should do some more work on our marriage, rather than working so hard on everything else. When is it ever going to stop? Besides, don't we watch too many videos instead of talking or doing something more creative?

Jason: We'll get caught up some day, won't we? Then we can have those kids we've been waiting for.

Betty: In time, Jason. We're still young. We've got a lot of things to work out first. I feel like I've got no energy. I'm always tired. All we ever do to relax is watch videos, or I watch TV while you play computer games. We just seem to be too exhausted to work on our marriage!

Jason: Well, we've got one good thing going for us—a good sex life!

Betty: Sex isn't everything, Jason. I think our marriage is just plain tired—we need some vitamins to revitalize it, or a whole new game plan. What do you think we could do?

Jason: Right now I suggest we get some sleep. Here we are—home. You go ahead into the apartment, I'll take out the trash for pickup tomorrow morning.

And so another Sunday ends; another week begins. The first step is taking out the trash.

Take a few moments to talk about the conversation of Betty and Jason. In what ways do they need to put more effort into their relationship? How might they do this?

Look into your partner's eyes and remember the love you saw there when you first fell in love. How has your love changed? Love is *always* changing, like the tides of the ocean. Now close your eyes and visualize yourself putting more energy and effort into this beautiful relationship—your marriage. How do you think you might do this? Look at each other and say, "Beginning today, I am going to put more energy into our relationship."

A Quick Marriage Energizer

1. Each of you will need a sheet of paper, an envelope, and a stamp.
2. Now, write a brief note of appreciation to your spouse. Start out something like this:

Dear _____,

I love you when you ... (hug me many times a day, bake my favorite pie, make that special coffee, bring me breakfast in bed on special occasions, spend time with me, do something that needs to be done around the house without being asked, listen to me when I feel down about work, etc.). Be creative!

3. Even if you have trouble writing notes, try to do it anyway; or buy a card, or find pictures from a magazine to make your own card.
4. Mail your note or card within the next week. Be sure it's a warm, positive note or card.

2. Your Energizing Quotient

Devotional Thought: "Christ encourages you, and his love comforts you. God's Spirit unites you. . . . Live in harmony by showing love for each other" (Philippians 2:1, 2 CEV).

So far, you have looked at your priorities, how you juggle your lives, and how you talk together. Now you are going to think about how you can energize your marriage.

Prayer: Lord, be with us now as we explore ways to energize our love and lives together. May we be open to new possibilities in our adventure of marriage. Amen.

What does it take to make your marriage the best it can be? Energy! You must put as much or more energy into your relationship—or "work," as it sometimes is described—as you put into jobs, hobbies, children, friends, and other relationships. If the "happily ever after" fairy-tale ending were a realistic concept of marriage, then there would be no need to put energy into your marriage. But the truth is that your life together will not be perfect. As you live together, you will encounter difficult or unpleasant situations and annoying habits that you may not have expected, and it will take energy to keep your promise to love for "better or worse." What makes this energy possible? Unconditional love and commitment.

Many times we are more loving to strangers and friends than we are to those we have promised to "love and cherish." We need to remember that just as God loves us unconditionally, so we are to love others unconditionally, *especially our spouses*—even when they forget to replace the toothpaste cap or leave their shoes in the middle of the floor or pile the dishes in the kitchen sink.

The focus of unconditional love should not be on ourselves—being accepted no matter what *we* do—but on our spouses—accepting them no matter what *they* do. In other words, rather than assuming that we can be our "worst selves" after marriage, as many couples do, we should try to be our "best selves." Rather than trying to change our spouses, we should try to change *ourselves*—those things we do that may "bug" or bother our spouses. This requires giving ourselves a regular "attitude check" and always striving not to be "jealous or proud, but...consider others [our spouses] more important than [ourselves]" (Philippians 2:3 CEV). How different this is from the widely accepted concept that "my needs" are most important!

Unconditional love is not a *given* of marriage; it, too, takes effort. That's where commitment comes in.

A recent magazine article suggested that the scariest moment in a marriage is not bringing the new baby home or losing a job, but wondering if you're "still in love." This moment came for the author of the article when, one day, he and his wife decided their relationship did not have the same "romantic intensity" it had when they were first married. They later discovered that in the act of loving each other, their love became real again. Sure, there were ups and downs, times of coasting and times of change, but by "hanging on" and remaining committed to each other and loving each other in very concrete ways, they were able to rekindle romance in their marriage and take their love to a more fulfilling depth.

Your circle of marriage is a cycle, beginning with love and commitment and continuing with more love and commitment. To keep this cycle going, you must

▲ view your marriage and your mate realistically;
▲ love each other unconditionally and forgive each other unreservedly;
▲ communicate, share, and negotiate in an honest and healthy way;
▲ take time to have fun together;
▲ continue to put energy into your relationship.

If you do these things, you will see growth and improvement in your marriage! Remember, remaining committed to making your marriage work and expressing your love for each other are what make a successful marriage. Unless you are willing to put energy into your relationship, your marriage will be stale and lifeless.

Your IQ is not the same today as it was when you took your first IQ test. It has been affected by many factors, such as education, experience, and environment. In the same way, your EQ, or energizing quotient, can change. Measuring your EQ is a good way to help you determine how you can begin to energize your marriage.

If possible, make a copy of the following exercise so that each of you may complete it separately. Otherwise, mark your responses in your notebooks. Plan to come back together after fifteen or twenty minutes, or if you finish ahead of time, check to see whether your spouse is done.

HOW'S YOUR EQ?

1. I place my marriage above other relationships and put as much or more energy into it than into other relationships in my life.

    _____ Most of the time   _____ Sometimes   _____ Not often

2. I try to put as much effort into speaking politely to my partner as I do into speaking politely to coworkers, friends, and acquaintances.

    _____ Most of the time   _____ Sometimes   _____ Not often

3. I do not put more energy into working, watching TV, playing computer games, or some other hobby or activity than I put into working on my marriage.

    _____ Most of the time   _____ Sometimes   _____ Not often

4. I try to comfort and nurture my mate when she/he needs me (is sad, lonely, discouraged, etc.).

    _____ Most of the time   _____ Sometimes   _____ Not often

5. I try to be romantic and sexually caring, and allow time for some "dating" to keep our physical intimacy growing.

    _____ Most of the time   _____ Sometimes   _____ Not often

6. If something about our relationship is bothering me, I express my concerns in a caring, loving way.

    _____ Most of the time   _____ Sometimes   _____ Not often

7. I try to change my habits or idiosyncrasies that may bother my partner.

    _____ Most of the time   _____ Sometimes   _____ Not often

8. Recognizing the frustrations of everyday life and the humanness of each of us, I try to be resilient and bounce back when I feel bad about something my spouse has said or done, without allowing these irritations to build up.

    _____ Most of the time   _____ Sometimes   _____ Not often

9. I realize that money, possessions, and prestige or honors cannot make up for an unhappy marriage.

    _____ Most of the time   _____ Sometimes   _____ Not often

10. I share openly and honestly and negotiate in a healthy way when making important decisions with my mate.

_____ Most of the time   _____ Sometimes   _____ Not often

11. I negotiate and share childrearing responsibilities and discipline with my partner.

_____ Most of the time   _____ Sometimes   _____ Not often

12. I am trying to relate God's unconditional love to my marriage by loving my spouse unconditionally.

_____ Most of the time   _____ Sometimes   _____ Not often

When you come back together, you might meet in the kitchen for a snack or light meal and share how each of you evaluated yourself. Or plan to go out to eat and take your evaluations with you. Then read on for ideas about how you can energize your marriage.

3. Ways to Energize Your Marriage

Devotional Thought: "Be quick to listen, slow to speak, slow to anger" (James 1:19); "If any think they are religious, and do not bridle their tongues . . . their religion is worthless" (James 1:26).

Remaining quiet, listening, and being tender are some of the most important ways to build and energize a marriage.

Prayer: God, help us to listen more and watch what we say as we look at ways to energize our marriage. Amen.

Ten Terrific Marriage Energizers

1. Relax Together.

It may seem contradictory to think about relaxing as you are trying to energize your marriage, but often it is the hustle and hurry of life that makes us tense and adds strain and stress to our marriages, as we discussed in chapter 2. In addition to breathing deeply and relaxing your body whenever you feel stress and tension, try to spend time relaxing as a couple on a regular basis. Here are a couple of ideas.

▲ As we suggested earlier, spend a few minutes greeting each other at the end of the day. Give each other a hug and kiss, talk casually (problems of the day are off-limits), and enjoy each other's company. The time you have for this will depend upon your family situation and schedule, but try to allow at least three to five minutes. If attending to young children's needs is not a consideration, allow as much as fifteen minutes. If possible, follow this time together with time to unwind separately. Read the paper, listen to music, take a bath, or do something else to relax. If you have been working with people or dealing with young children all day, you may need to have a "quiet time" or go for a walk. If it is not possible for each of you to do this simultaneously, take turns. Once each of you has had the opportunity to unwind—even if only for a few minutes—you will have more energy to share *together*.

▲ Create a place or small space where the two of you can go to relax together. It might be two facing seats in the living room, a blanket under a tree in your yard, or a bench in a nearby park. You might have several places. Wherever it is, it should be a place where you can relax, unwind, "cool down," and find peace—no arguing allowed!

2. Treat your spouse nicely.

It is sad but true: Many people are nice to everyone they meet—the checkout clerk at the supermarket, the newspaper carrier, a friend they've known for years or only a short time, coworkers, and others—except their spouses! Sometimes the buildup of the day's activities, anger about a work situation, an upsetting conversation with a friend or relative, or even minor irritations can lead to an evening of "everything and anything goes." Who gets dumped on? That's right, the one you love so much. Again, it is so important to take time to relax before talking about the problems of the day. Not only in the evening but whenever you are together, be careful not to take out your frustrations on your mate. And don't forget common courtesies, such as "Please," "Thank-you," "Would you mind if...?" and "I would really appreciate it if...." Treat the special someone in your life as nicely as you treat anyone else. Does it take effort? Of course! Doesn't everything worthwhile take effort?

3. Practice resiliency.

Resiliency is the way we bounce back from something that bothers us. How well do you bounce back? Decide how you will do this.

▲ Tell your spouse what is bothering you: "I am really bothered by..." or "I would like you to...."

▲ If the incident is minor, acknowledge that it upsets you, but don't let it spoil your whole day or week, as often happens when something goes wrong. It's a good idea to "time yourself" to see how long something bothers you, trying to decrease the length of time with each bothersome situation.

4. Make time to have fun together.

Ask yourself questions such as these: "Who or what is taking most of my energy? Work? A friend? The telephone? A hobby? The TV? The computer? Does it deserve more energy than I am giving my spouse? How can I change this? Limit TV or computer time? Do I really need to work so much overtime? Is it possible to bring some work home—or to stop bringing work home? Am I a workaholic? Too ambitious for money or advancement? Is this hurting my marriage?" After thinking about what "energy takers" you need to eliminate, consider the following ways to spend time enjoying each other.

▲ When do each of you go to bed? Get up in the morning? If one of you is a morning bird and the other is a night owl, how about cuddling together at night or in the morning before keeping your own "time schedules"? Believe it or not, it is possible to adapt to the other's schedule, morning or night, and even to become a morning *and* night person. But be careful, you might lose a lot of sleep that way!

▲ If your schedules make it hard to adapt, each week plan to do something one of you likes, alternating who chooses the activity. One week you might want to bake brownies, make popcorn, go to a museum, or do something else your spouse is not so crazy about. The next week your spouse gets to choose the activity!

▲ Start a "couple custom." Play a game you both enjoy once a week. Tennis, Scrabble, cards, checkers—it doesn't matter. Fun is the idea! Have lunch together once a week or once a month. Have an annual Christmas tree decorating party just for the two of you—or with children and others—and serve hot chocolate and cookies. (If you're too busy to make cookies, buy them! Don't get into the Christmas rush syndrome!) The possibilities are endless. Read on for more ideas.

5. Rekindle romance.

Do you need to "spice up" your romantic life and put more energy into it? We will cover this in detail in chapter 5. For now, here are a few ideas you might try.

▲ Plan at least one date a month—without the children. This togetherness time is extremely important to the intimacy of your marriage.

▲ Go away for a weekend—just the two of you. Make arrangements for an overnight getaway at a local hotel featuring special weekend rates or a nearby bed and breakfast. Save for this if your budget is tight. You'll be making an investment in your marriage.

▲ Once a week, light a candle in the evening—after the children have gone to bed—for a time of prayer and/or romance. Yes, the two can go together!

▲ Write frequent "love notes" to each other. Tuck one in a lunch bag, attach one to the refrigerator, tape one to the bathroom mirror, send one to your spouse at work via E-mail—use your imagination!

6. Nurture and comfort each other.

When your mate comes to you needing comfort—because of problems at work, relationships, or physical illness—do you comfort her or him? When your mate needs encouragement to try new visions, do you listen and try to give support if possible? Most of all, do you listen lovingly and tenderly?

One wife said, "My husband doesn't have to 'fix things' or 'tell me what to do'; all he has to do is hold me, put his arm around me, or touch me gently, showing that he understands how I feel." By simply showing that you care and by listening attentively, you will give your spouse the comfort she or he needs.

7. Value your spouse.

Ask yourself, "Do I value my spouse above position, possessions, and honors? Do I treat my loved one as the most valued treasure of all I have?" Often couples do value each other, but they fail to verbalize it or show it in concrete ways. One of the most effective ways you can demonstrate that you value your spouse is to compliment him or her in public. Try it and see what happens!

8. Share your faith together.

Do you look to God for help in energizing your relationship? Do you follow Jesus' example and teachings, which help you to know how to have the most meaningful relationship with your mate? Do you pray for guidance—alone and together? Do you worship God together, talk about your faith together, and read or study the Bible together? If you have children, do you share the responsibility of teaching the faith to your children?

9. Talk about your family of origin.

The examples we witness as children have a dramatic and lasting impact on us. Even as adults, we often find ourselves repeating behaviors or patterns we observed in one or both of our parents. Perhaps your parents were not as loving or polite or tender with each other as they should have been. Sometimes you may find yourself being extra critical or withdrawing or refusing to talk when you really don't want to act that way. Perhaps your parents or the parents of several of your friends divorced when you were young. You may find yourself thinking that if things don't work out in your marriage, you will simply get a divorce. Overcoming these tendencies takes effort, but talking about your families and sharing your feelings can help you to better understand each other.

Within each of us is the "child" who loves to have fun, and we must keep this child. But there also may be within us the "child" who is hurt or sad. Sometimes the love, care, and nurture of our mates can help us to acknowledge and deal with this more easily. If, however, experiences and/or relationships from your childhood are causing serious problems for you or your marriage, you may need to seek professional help.

10. Practice forgiveness.

Do you say "I'm sorry" when you have done something to hurt or annoy your spouse? Then do you talk about it or try to change it? Are you careful not to say "I'm sorry" without meaning it or simply as a routine response? If you have seriously wronged your mate, do you need to talk to a pastor or counselor about how to seek forgiveness and get past this barrier in your relationship?

Pastors, counselors, and therapists generally agree that "confessing" all the sins of the past—especially serious ones—may not be helpful to a relationship. You may want to get something off your chest, but this actually might be hurtful to your mate. If you need to make such a confession, make an appointment to talk to a pastor or Christian counselor about it.

Often, because of past sins, we burden ourselves with "false guilt" about little things for which we do not need to feel guilty. On the other hand, we must be sure that our conscience—God's voice within—is intact and that we listen to it! The important thing we must never forget is that God forgives us. Sometimes it's harder to forgive ourselves than it is to understand and accept the forgiveness of God.

Does your mate need forgiveness? Don't forget or refuse to forgive, for this brings healing to any relationship. Are there people from your past, such as family members or others, whom you need to forgive within yourself—when it might not be appropriate to express your forgiveness in person?

Do *you* need forgiveness? Confess your sin to God—and to others, if appropriate—and accept God's unconditional forgiveness.

————————————

Jason and Betty learned a lesson of forgiveness that helped them to begin energizing their marriage at the same time. It was 10:00 P.M. on Friday evening, one week after their trip to see Betty's parents. Jason was just coming home from his job at the video store. Betty was folding laundry. Their conversation went something like this: (Read this aloud as if you are Betty and Jason.)

Betty: I'm glad to see you, honey. I've been lonely tonight. Can you give me a hand with some of this?

Jason: Sure, I'll take care of the towels.

Betty: Where are the videos you usually bring home for the weekend?

Jason: I didn't bring any home.

Betty: You forgot?

Jason: No, I just decided not to bring any.

Betty: Why?

Jason: After our talk last week, I've been thinking that maybe you're right. In a way, watching videos has been our escape from each other. I'm sorry, Betty, for the way this whole video thing started. I think that was mostly my fault. I thought it would help you feel better about me working there, and I guess I was kind of scared to take time out to work on things that I'm not so good at discussing.

Betty: It's really not your fault, Jason. I'm sorry for the way I've been acting lately—like I'm just too tired to do much about our lifestyle. I guess I've been more intent on keeping in touch with my family on the phone when we're not visiting them. I never should have compared you to my brother and some of the things he can do. I love you more than anyone in the world. Forgive me for complaining so much. Besides, you do a lot of things better than Bob.

Jason: Thanks. I'm sorry, too, for always bringing up "having children" when I know you may not be ready yet.

Betty: I'm so glad you didn't bring the videos home. Let's not watch any for a while. Maybe we can start to put some of that energy into our marriage, like we used to when we were dating—before we got into the rut of every week being the same.

Jason: Hey, I've got a great idea!

Betty: Could you tell me about it over a dish of heavenly hash ice cream?

Jason: That's even better! Let's "hash over" all the ways we can work on "us" that we can think of! It'll be like a game. You name one, then I'll name one, and the one who names the most ideas wins!

Betty: No, we both win! And our marriage wins!

Why don't you spend some time brainstorming your own list of ways you can energize your marriage—individually and together. Complete the following sentences:

Wife: I will try to put more energy into our marriage in these ways:	Husband: I will try to put more energy into our marriage in these ways:
1.	1.
2.	2.
3.	3.
4.	4.
5.	5.

Read this poem as a prayer to end your time of sharing:

The Secret Is "Energized"

Here we are together—as husband and wife,
Looking at ways to give zest to our life.
During this time we both have realized
That our marriage needs to be energized!

Life has been good, but we want something more,
And we know that it can't be bought at a store.
It's a matter of getting our thoughts synchronized,
As we recognize our marriage must be energized!

We agree that whatever we do—whatever we say
Must be shared with love—it's the only way!
And when all the plans we make are finalized
Our marriage will thrive—only as it's energized!

When we glance back to see what we have done
From the dawn of the day 'til the setting sun,
We will find that we are blessed and often surprised
To see how God helped our marriage to be energized!

This is our prayer, O God. Amen.

5. KEEPING THE SPARK ALIVE

▼

"It only takes a spark to get a fire going." These words from the opening line of a beautiful song about God's love, and how we share it, also describe the igniting effect of love between a husband and wife. Such a love, once it's burning brightly, warms the thoughts and the heart, initiating physical impulses to express the intense joy of sharing life fully, and the awareness that God intended for us to be joined together in such a bond of oneness.

The spark of romantic love is essential to ignite the blaze of physical intimacy in marriage, just as a glowing ember is essential to ignite a blaze of all-consuming flame in a fireplace on a cold, wintry night. Yet for some couples after several years of marriage, the spark of romantic love becomes nothing more than a smoldering ember. For others, it seems to have been completely extinguished.

When the spark of romance is cooling or missing from a marriage, is there hope to ignite it again? Of course there is! How? By taking a close look at what was, what is now, and what could be.

1. When the Spark Ignited

Jim and Nancy are in their seventh year of marriage. They have what could be described as a very good marriage. They have defined their priorities. They juggle their activities and responsibilities without too much stress. They talk together and are energized for all they must do, giving the outward appearance that they are having a good time while doing it. They are financially stable and their children are healthy and seem well adjusted. They work together on projects, worship together in church, attend community functions together, and volunteer when possible. They get enough sleep, take vitamins, get adequate exercise, and keep in touch with relatives in ways beyond what might be expected. Life is good!

Yet something is missing: the spark of romantic love, the warmth and passion of an all-consuming love. The feeling of wanting each other more than anything else in the world has faded into an occasional recall or replay, as they review photos from earlier years.

Jim and Nancy were considered the most romantic couple on their college campus, where they met during their sophomore year. During their junior year, they were together almost constantly—walking to classes, holding hands, sharing long, lingering kisses in secluded places. The sparkle in their eyes reflected the spark of love that had ignited in their hearts.

In those days, they were both great dancers and loved romantic music. They enjoyed going to movies together, watching football games together, and studying in the library together; but they never slept together, even though many of their friends did. Sex was to be saved for marriage—an ethic and discipline taught in both their homes. Their sexual desire for each other was the hardest thing to keep under control, especially for Jim; but they did wait.

Their wedding day arrived, and their honeymoon was an explosion of passion. The spark of love was continually fanned into flame. It was an incredible week—exploring, discovering, enjoying, expressing the depth of their love in ways they had never experienced. They returned home with a glow that was evident to all.

What happened, then?

Before continuing the story of Jim and Nancy's love life—or lack thereof—pause to reflect on your own special moments of romance and "lovemaking." Talk openly about how you truly felt in those moments.

Share this devotional thought thanking God for bringing you together.

Devotional Thought: "Let him kiss me with the kisses of his mouth! . . . Ah, you are beautiful, my love; ah, you are beautiful" (Song of Solomon 1:2a, 15).

Prayer: Thank you, God, for the warmth of my beloved's kiss and the spark of love that brought us together. Help us to keep it burning. Amen.

---

2. What Causes the Spark to Lose Its Glow?

As they entered into a new chapter called "married life" and followed the example of both sets of parents, Jim and Nancy settled into a routine of establishing goals, saving for a house, planning a family, working hard all week, and making love on Saturday nights. At first, the spark remained, yet other priorities seemed to crowd out time for being romantic. Not only was there less time to make love, but the tender touches and little surprises that had been so special when they were dating were fading into a blur of "what used to be."

Becky was born ten months after their wedding day, and Jimmy followed two years later, after which they agreed that two children were enough. Parenting seemed to take almost all their time at home. Privacy in their bedroom was never enforced—or intended. They agreed that the children should be able to enter whenever they wished. Otherwise, they thought, the children might feel rejected. Becky and Jimmy were part of everything. They were "one big happy family."

Slowly, the Saturday-night spark was ignited into flame less frequently. "What if the children aren't asleep yet?" they would say. As far as they knew, their parents had lived the same way.

For some reason, other romantic thoughts and expressions seemed to slip out of focus as the frequency of their sexual encounters diminished. The urges were still there, but the spark to initiate something, to proceed to the fulfillment of lovemaking, was missing. With the exception of holding hands in public, they had few other romantic expressions.

The thought of going out on a date or spending a weekend somewhere together never seemed to enter their minds, even when friends talked about the great times they had away from their children. When others asked why they didn't take some time away for themselves, Jim and Nancy usually answered, "While the children are young, we want them to be with us and share some weekends away as a family." (We will discuss this perspective further in chapter 8.)

By the time they reached their seventh year of marriage, this philosophy of family togetherness had become routine. After all, they thought, isn't that the way married couples should live—being good friends and good parents?

Whether the situation of Jim and Nancy sounds familiar or is far from your own experience, it is important to talk together about the romantic spark in your marriage. Take time now to examine your own romantic expressions, beginning with the role models of your parents and the effect these may have had on your love life. Be honest but not judgmental as you reflect on the ways your mother and father—or stepparent—expressed romantic love. If you had only one parent or were raised by someone other than a parent, you might reflect on some important role models in your life, such as grandparents, an aunt and uncle, the parents of a friend or schoolmate, or a couple in your church or neighborhood.

If possible, make a copy of the following checklist; otherwise, one or both of you may mark your responses in a notebook. As each of you consider the ways you observed your parents—or other role models—demonstrating their affection for each other, check the appropriate boxes.

Romance Role Models

I remember my parents (or other role models)

YES	NO		NOT SURE
☐	☐	Kissing each other "hello" and/or "good-bye"	☐
☐	☐	Touching, holding hands	☐

☐	☐	Giving hugs and holding each other close	☐
☐	☐	Saying "I love you" to each other frequently	☐
☐	☐	Sitting together on the sofa (with an arm around one or the other) reading or watching TV	☐
☐	☐	Going out on a date on a regular basis	☐
☐	☐	Surprising each other with little gifts	☐
☐	☐	Spending an occasional weekend away together	☐
☐	☐	Closing the bedroom door for times of love-making (at least you assumed that this was happening)	☐
☐	☐	Spending time together—perhaps listening to romantic music or looking through scrapbooks or photo albums—and reminiscing about their courtship or early years of marriage	☐

Other expressions:

Next, consider the ways the two of you *currently* express your affection for each other, working together to complete the following checklist.

OUR MARRIAGE TODAY

We share our affection by

YES	NO		NOT SURE
☐	☐	Kissing each other "hello" and/or "good-bye"	☐
☐	☐	Touching, holding hands	☐
☐	☐	Giving hugs and holding each other close	☐
☐	☐	Saying "I love you" to each other frequently	☐
☐	☐	Sitting together on the sofa (with an arm around one or the other) reading or watching TV	☐
☐	☐	Going out on a date on a regular basis	☐
☐	☐	Surprising each other with little gifts	☐
☐	☐	Spending an occasional weekend away together	☐

Now compare the checklists of your parents' or other role models' romantic expressions with your own checklist. How do you see romance in your marriage in relation to their marriages? What traits or expressions of theirs have become a part of your lives and your expression of love for each other? Do you see more positive or negative effects from their relationships in your marriage? How might you change any of the negative effects, so that they do not become a self-fulfilling prophecy for you? What specific things can you do to shift your "no" responses to the "yes" column? Talk for a few minutes about these questions, trying to be fair as you reflect on similarities and differences between your marriage and those of your parents or other role models.

What other factors may be causing the spark in your marriage to lose its glow? Are there other changes you need to make? As you continue talking, allow yourselves to laugh together and even cry together, if you need to. Most of all, listen carefully to each other.

Before continuing your discussion of romance in your marriage, take a moment to ask God to guide you into the future.

Devotional Thought: "Now we see in a mirror, dimly, but then we will see face to face. Now I know only in part; then I will know fully, even as I have been fully known" (1 Corinthians 13:12).

Prayer: Dear God, As we glance into the mirror of the past, we sometimes see images of our parents or others blurred into our own reflections. Help us to be grateful for the ways they have helped us grow in love and to overlook the ways their examples may have restricted our own expression of sexual intimacy and romance. Help us to understand more fully what love can truly mean, and guide us to see clearly the beauty and joy you intend for us—to be "one" together in body and spirit. Amen.

3. Fanning the Flame

Sexual Intimacy

 Though certainly not the only contributor to intimacy and romance, the sexual relationship plays a very important role in marriage. Sexuality is God's good gift, intended to unite two persons physically, emotionally, and spiritually in the marriage relationship. Sexuality offers us an opportunity to express love in one of the most beautiful ways possible, even as God's love has been expressed to us and through us in ongoing creativity. In many ways, sexuality is creativity—exploring the meaning of giving and receiving love, as a woman and a man "become one" in physical expressions, symbolic of their spiritual oneness.

Whenever a sexual relationship becomes an "end in and of itself," the gift of sexuality is being used for self-gratification, rather than as an expression of giving oneself fully to one's spouse. When a sexual relationship is an act of *giving*, however, it also becomes an experience of *receiving*. As an expression of God's creative love in each of us, sexuality is to be continually explored, understood, and shared in marriage, in ways that couples agree upon together.

Let's tune in to Jim and Nancy once more. It is Sunday evening, after the children are in bed, and Jim and Nancy are talking about the class discussion they had at church this morning. After hearing a guest speaker on the theme "How to Keep the Romance in Your Marriage," the couples in the class talked about their determination to put more romance back into their marriages.

As you read their conversation aloud, assume the roles of Nancy and Jim. Try to put yourselves into their feelings as you read. Let the dialogue come alive!

Nancy: Do you think our marriage needs more romance, Jim?

Jim: I didn't think so before this morning, but maybe we do. I remember when we could hardly keep our hands off each other.

Nancy: I miss those days, Jim. I guess I didn't realize how much until now. We both seem happy, but we don't do the little things we used to—like you giving me little surprises and taking me somewhere I didn't expect. I loved those times!

Jim: You used to surprise me, too. And you had a way of "turning me on"—and I don't mean just in bed, but other times, too—with the sexy outfits you used to wear.

Nancy: We've changed, somehow, and I guess we've let ourselves forget how it used to be.

Jim: But at least we make love.

Nancy: Yes, but not very often.

Jim: Well, I'm ready whenever you are!

Nancy: You make it sound as if I'm not ready—and sometimes I'm not, Jim. You can't just say, "Let's do it." I miss the tender touches, the slow, romantic approach. I know you're tired at the end of the day, but it doesn't always have to be the end of the day.

Jim: I guess you're right. I either move too quickly or not at all with sex. You know, I never saw my father show much tenderness with my mom, either, although I'm sure he loved her.

Nancy: My parents were kind of the same way. My mother wasn't exactly romantic. She did her thing and let Dad do his. They didn't spend much time together alone.

Jim: Maybe we're falling into the same trap. How can we change things?

Nancy: We'll have to be more flexible—without scheduling everything so tightly. It's so easy to get in a rut.

Jim: It's funny. I'm really creative at work, but I haven't thought about being romantically creative.

(They continue to undress, getting ready for bed.)

Nancy: Maybe we could start by wearing something sexy to bed. Remember those bikini shorts I gave you one Valentine's Day a couple of years ago?

Jim: You mean the ones with little red hearts and the words "Be mine"?

Nancy: You never wore those, did you?

Jim: I thought they were just a fun gift.

Nancy: Fun is the whole idea! But they're no fun unless you wear them for me!

Jim: I think they're still here in the dresser. You mean these?

Nancy: Try them on!

Jim: Now?

Nancy: Why not?

Jim: I guess I'm a little embarrassed, even with you.

Nancy: I wouldn't be embarrassed if you bought some special things for me to wear.

Jim: You mean at a women's lingerie store?

Nancy: Sure, lots of men do that.

Jim: Well, maybe I will too!

Nancy: You're on!

Jim: Okay, but for right now, just close your eyes a minute.

Nancy closed her eyes while Jim took off the rest of his clothes and slipped into the "Be Mine" bikini shorts with red hearts. At first they laughed, but the shorts had a "turn on" effect for Nancy, and the rest of the night was filled with more passion than they could remember.

Talk together about the conversation between Jim and Nancy. How did each of you feel as you spoke their words? Do you ever feel the same way as

Jim or Nancy? Perhaps you might begin by reflecting on those times when you have felt best about sharing sex; then talk together about what made those times special. What was the setting (where and when)? Was it after a "date"? What were your surroundings? Was there music? A fire crackling in a fireplace?

Now pretend you are on a deserted island covered in tropical foliage and trees, with delectable ripened fruit. The sun is warm, yet a gentle breeze cools you as the tide comes in ever so gradually on the sandy beach. There is only the sound of birds and rustling leaves. You are alone, secure, fearless, and completely uninhibited. What will you do? What will you say?

As you think of other creative ways to explore this aspect of your marriage, try not to be critical of each other. Remember that it is best to talk about your sexual expressions and any concerns you may have at times other than when making love—such as while sharing lunch or dinner (just the two of you!) or when reviewing your total life together.

It is also important to communicate with each other in other ways *during* times of lovemaking. Recognizing that men and women often have different attitudes and expectations about sex, we offer the following as examples that many husbands and wives might find helpful. Of course, depending upon the individuals and their particular needs, each of these statements may be appropriate for one or both partners.

A wife might say:
"I like it when you kiss me that way," or "I like it when you do that."
"I like to cuddle and hug like this before we make love."
"Could we take it just a little slower? I'm not quite ready."
"I like it when you talk to me and hold me before going to sleep."
"I really want to talk a little about what happened today first."

A husband might say:
"I really like it when you kiss me that way," or "I like it when you do that."
"Would you...?" or "Let's try something different." (If the other person hesitates, this is something that may need to be discussed at another time.)

Remember, it is always better to discuss concerns or problems at times other than when making love. Some common concerns or issues you may need to discuss at some point in your married life include physical problems; differing needs, preferences, and rates of arousal; and any related emotional concerns. Some couples may discover that they need professional help in one or more areas—from a medical doctor, therapist, or counselor. Never hesitate or be ashamed to seek the help *you* need to keep your own sexual relationship alive and healthy.

Pause now to thank God for the joy of sexual intimacy you share as husband and wife.

Devotional Thought: "My beloved speaks and says to me: 'Arise, my love, my fair one, and come away'" (Song of Solomon 2:10).

Prayer: Thank you, God, for the times we have experienced that special "burning desire" to share love together, and for the ecstasy of fulfillment when we have been "one with each other." We are aware that such love is part of your plan for a wife and husband, and that is why you created us for each other. Amen.

Other Ways of Expressing Love

Although sexual intimacy is a very important way to express love in marriage, there are many other ways to say "I love you." In fact, without these other romantic expressions, a couple's sexual relationship generally suffers. After all, it is the little sparks of romance that lead to the burning flames of passion.

The following exercise describes some of these expressions of love. It is intended to help each of you "keep in touch" with what your spouse enjoys. If possible, make a copy of the checklist; otherwise, one or both of you may mark your responses in a notebook. Check those items that you think would appeal especially to your mate, not necessarily to yourself—although you will realize that if your mate truly enjoys these things, you will receive pleasure too. Add any others you think should be included. Complete the exercise without sharing.

HOW WELL DO YOU KNOW YOUR MATE?

My mate enjoys/would enjoy

☐ holding hands   ☐ finding a love note on the pillow

☐ going for a walk together   ☐ being surprised with a gift or special treat

☐ dancing   ☐ hearing "I love you"

☐ making love   ☐ making dinner or a favorite dessert together

☐ receiving flowers   ☐ receiving compliments on his/her looks

☐ taking a shower together   ☐ receiving compliments on his/her achievements

---

☐ being read to	☐ having dinner out
☐ getting a backrub	☐ having the bed turned down for him/her
☐ having me initiate sex	☐ having me express interest in his/ her special pasttime
☐ Others _____	

When both of you are finished, talk about the choices you made for your mate and why you selected these things. Was either of you surprised by what your spouse thought you would find pleasurable? Are there things you would enjoy that your spouse did not select? Discuss what you have discovered about each other and how you might explore and expand some of these very special expressions of love. Be creative!

> WHY BE ROMANTIC?
> To revive your relationship.
> To improve the quality of your life.
> To help you fall in love all over again!

To help get your creative juices flowing, here are some possibilities adapted from *1001 Ways to Be Romantic* by Gregory J. P. Godek. As you read the list, circle those you might like to try sometime.

▲ Create some custom romance coupons: backrub coupons, lovemaking coupons, music tape/CD coupons, and so forth.

▲ Go for a horse-drawn carriage ride through the city—or the country.

▲ Bring home Chinese food for dinner. Replace the paper in your mate's fortune cookie with a custom-made fortune you write yourself!

▲ When you're going to be away from home, tape your photo to your pillow where your mate will find it.

▲ Record "your song" on cassette tape and gift wrap it. Then give it to your mate!

▲ Fake a power outage. (Loosen the fuses or throw the switch.) No TV. Just candlelight. Now—use your imagination.

▲ Order a pizza. Get the pizza chef to arrange the pepperoni in the shape of a heart.

▲ Go for a walk. Go to a ballgame. Go hiking. Go on a picnic. Go tobogganing. Go for it!

▲ Go shopping for a "love gift." Rather than looking for a specific item, let the gift find *you!*

▲ *Listen*—with your ears, mind, and heart. Listen for the meaning behind his actions. Listen for the message behind her words.

▲ Write one page on one of these topics: *I love you because...; or I remember when we first met....*

▲ Loosen those purse strings. Loosen your schedule. Loosen your *attitude.*

▲ Don't wait until Saturday night to go out dancing! *Dance by yourselves at home in your living room!*

▲ Breakfast in bed is nice—but how about having *dinner* in bed!

▲ Recapture the fun in your romantic relationship. We adults are *much* too serious *much* too often!

These are only suggestions. Try to think of as many others as you can. Remember, surprise is the key to some of the happiest romantic moments.

A Few Reminders

Always remember special days—each other's birthday and your wedding anniversary. Celebrate these times with advance planning, whether a simple gift, a homemade card, one flower, or a delightful dinner (just the two of you), and possibly overnight in a romantic setting (especially on your anniversary). Be imaginative.

As you reflect on how you can express your love to each other, remember that love is expressed in many different ways. Sometimes the way will be a tender touch, an unexpected gift, or a brief note. Other times it will be a moment of intense passion, culminating in the complete release of inner feelings and a burning desire that words cannot define. Likewise, the spark is not always ignited in the same way. There is no checklist of specific suggestions that, if followed, will work for everyone. Every couple is unique. Romantic love is your own expression. No one can tell you exactly what to do or when and where to do it, though many "experts" may try—such as those who suggest that one position is the secret for sexual ecstasy. There is no book, magazine article, or lecture that will provide all the answers. You must be creative, be yourselves, and experiment with romance.

Here are a few final suggestions for you to think about and discuss as you conclude this time together:

1. Always be completely open to the ideas your spouse may have about specific romantic expressions. Do not discard any suggestion that either of you may express, unless it is offensive or hurtful in some way.

2. Light a candle together in the darkness. This can provide more than symbolic meaning. Love is like a candle. The flickering flame of candlelight creates warm emotions and continuing creativity—never the same.

3. Look into each other's eyes with a feeling beyond words; speak the words you want to share. Listen with total awareness. Touch with a tenderness that combines caressing with the mystery of God's creation of your bodies.

4. Focus on a flower. This does not mean buying expensive bouquets of flowers, or surprising your spouse with flowers only on special occasions. Giving even one flower can speak so much in wonder and beauty. Remember, love is like a flower. Just as a rosebud opens to full splendor, so also your love can be fulfilled.

5. Let there be joy, laughter, smiles! Life is meant to be "joy-full." Love is an expression of joy—in creation and in the delight of the Creator. Joy is the promise of the One who came to show us how to love each other unconditionally. "These things have I spoken to you, that my joy might remain in you, and that your joy might be full" (John 15:11 KJV).

Now, hold each other close and say to each other, "I love you. I love you. I love you." Seal your love with a kiss!

6. FOR RICHER OR POORER

▼

"For richer or poorer." These words continue to be part of the wedding vows—along with words such as "for better or worse" and "in sickness and in health"—under the overarching phrase "to love and to cherish." As husband and wife, you are to love and cherish each other whether you are "rich" or "poor"—or somewhere in between. This is part of the covenant of marriage.

When viewed as a resource that God has allowed us to share, money is a positive factor and influence in marriage. Indeed, it is essential for meeting the needs of daily living. It provides not only physical necessities but also a quality of life that contributes to a sense of security—having enough rather than existing in a continual state of anxiety about undergirding the family financially. Many couples find that the quality of their marriage is enhanced when they feel *adequate* in terms of managing their money—regardless of the amount they have to manage.

Unfortunately, some couples allow money to create an image of success or failure within their marriage, especially in the early years when they may compare their financial assets with those of friends, relatives, and other couples they know. Often these couples view money as a symbol of status or self-worth, believing their value is determined by their ability to purchase visible signs of their success—cars, houses, furniture, clothing, electronic/technical equipment. Even the brand names of such items are considered status symbols as couples are tempted to impress their friends and excel in comparison to others in the community.

In such marriages, however, there is the distinct danger that money can become a goal in and of itself—regardless of how it is used. This sometimes occurs without marriage partners fully realizing it. Yet when "love of money" replaces love for others and love for God, money becomes "the root of all evil" (1 Timothy 6:10).

When one or both partners are obsessed with money and the things money can buy, the expression of their love diminishes as the obsession intensifies. Such an obsession with money can become an all-consuming passion to build up financial reserves so that a bank account will reflect an ever-larger balance and offset any need that might arise. The passion for acquiring more and more money tends to push aside the passion for simply loving each other—and loving those values inherent in "who one is," rather than how much one owns.

In many relationships, money means power. If one partner earns a large portion of the family income, for example, often this becomes a symbol of power and control. The partner with the greater earning power may expect to control all decisions about spending and saving, frequently exhibiting a judgmental attitude as well.

It is very important for couples to see themselves as a team when it comes to managing their marriage, especially as they focus on financial matters and decisions related to prioritizing their needs and budgeting to meet these needs. Partnership is vital to the success of any financial plan a couple might have, particularly as it affects their respect for each other and their commitment to reach goals that require financial support.

Sharing responsibility for managing money does not mean that one partner will not have greater knowledge or expertise than the other; it does mean that the partners will respect each other's views and abilities. (It is important, however, that both wife and husband have a basic knowledge of all monetary accounts, in the event that one partner should be separated from the other.) This requires a genuine willingness to work together to resolve concerns and reach decisions that will enhance the well-being and future security of the family.

Money is one of the most frequently listed causes of marital problems, yet there are underlying issues "masked" by dollar signs! This chapter is not intended to solve all of a couple's monetary concerns. There are many helpful books that deal with money management and specific money problems, some of which are listed in the bibliography.

The primary purpose of this chapter is to identify some of the problems that couples face when focusing on money and, more specifically, to help you think about your specific needs related to managing your resources. Most important is the recognition that God can help you find some of these answers through a careful, prayerful review of your financial needs in the total context of your family's life. It is this basic belief in God's faithfulness and goodness that provides a sense of wealth beyond a bank account.

1. Our Money Concerns

Do you consider yourself financially secure—"rich enough"? Or are you on the other side of the ledger, facing seemingly impossible demands on your family income and considering yourself "poor" or "in need"? Perhaps you're somewhere in the middle, being able to meet your basic needs but struggling to feel that you have enough. Regardless of how you might describe your financial state, the truth may be that you have money concerns—not about the amount of money you have, but about the way you and your spouse discuss and/or handle your finances. The first step in addressing these concerns is to identify them *together*.

Carol and Bob are a young couple struggling to stay financially solvent as they plan for the future. They come from families with quite different views of money. Carol's family could be described as affluent by most standards. There always seemed to be enough money for whatever was needed—including her college tuition—although her mother and father argued frequently about financial matters. Bob's family, on the other hand, continually faced financial crises. Bob worked to help pay his way through college, in addition to taking out student loans, which he repaid in full only a year ago. After meeting Carol, he wanted somehow to provide for her and their future family in the same way she always had been provided for.

Carol and Bob have been married for five years and have one son, Robbie, who is three. Carol, now four months pregnant, works part time as a computer programmer. Bob works for the State Highway Administration—an office job that he dislikes but that has a good salary and benefits. Two cats also occupy the house they are renting with option to purchase.

Let's look in on Bob and Carol, who are away for two nights while Robbie stays with grandparents. They accepted an offer to check out a time-share condominium community, with all expenses paid as part of a promotional plan. The promotional literature assured them that their only responsibilities would be to take a ninety-minute tour and listen to a thirty-minute presentation; they would not be required to purchase anything. Actually, they had no intention of buying into the plan because they wouldn't be able to afford it. The free weekend sounded like a good deal, and they simply couldn't resist the offer, since they hadn't been away together for over a year.

It is about eight o'clock in the evening. Earlier in the day they took the tour and heard the lecture. Now they have just returned from dinner to their attractively decorated guest quarters. As they sit together on the love seat in the spacious bedroom, they are looking over the promotional brochures they were given. Read their parts aloud, putting yourselves into the conversation.

Bob: You know, this whole plan looks so neat. I wish we could buy into one of these lower-cost weeks. Couldn't we reconsider our decision?

Carol: You can't be serious, Bob! There's no way we can afford to put that much money down—plus make the monthly payments!

Bob: But just think what a great place this would be for the future. Jim and Kay have a time-share, and they keep saying what a good deal it is.

Carol: Well, let's think about it after we're better established and can save some for Robbie's schooling? There are also the costs of the baby coming, and I won't be able to go back to work, even part time, for several months.

Bob: Our insurance should cover all the costs of the baby, and we do have some money in savings for other expenses and for Robbie. I know what you're saying is true, Carol, I just feel bad not being able to invest in something we'd enjoy so much through the years. Sometimes I feel as if we're poor compared to our friends.

Carol: Bob, we're not poor! I don't feel that way at all. I guess I'm just more realistic about money than you are. We should have more in our savings account. If we don't, we won't be prepared for emergencies. My parents always taught us to save for the future.

Bob: And what have your parents done with all the money they've saved?

Carol: Well, they've gone on a couple of trips—once to Alaska, and last winter to New Orleans.

Bob: But that's all they've done, Carol. They saved so much through the years, and yet never seemed to enjoy life. Now that your father has so much trouble with his arthritis, they don't go anywhere. They sit around the house watching TV and cutting out coupons for groceries. They didn't seem to really enjoy life when they could have. I don't want our life to be that way!

Carol: My parents were trying to do the best they could for the family. I don't think it's fair for you to criticize them. We can probably learn from both of our families, but let's not put them down. Let's see what we can do and understand that it's in our hands. It's our decision.

Bob: Maybe we need to take another look at how we can spend our time and money to really enjoy life.

Carol: I agree, and I want us to have a good time looking at the possibilities. But I have to confess that even though my parents did save a lot of money, they were always arguing about it. My father had the checkbook, and he always accused my mother of spending too much. They couldn't agree on any big purchases, especially Christmas presents. I remember sitting on the stairs one night, listening as they argued about how much to spend on each of us. After a while, we kids didn't even want any presents if it was going to cause that much of a problem!

Bob: My parents weren't perfect, either. They argued about lots of things, but not about money. We just didn't have enough. Then came Vietnam, and you know what happened. Dad never came home. Mom's been pretty well cared for with the insurance money, but she often said, "I'd rather have your dad than the money." She's lonely, you know.

Carol: That's one thing I hope I never have to experience. I need you, Bob. Maybe it's good that we came here. We're getting into some things we might not have talked about otherwise. Let me ask you something. What would you do if you had all the money you would ever need?

Bob: I'd buy you everything you could possibly imagine—after giving 10 percent to the church!

Carol: You really were listening to the pastor's sermon on stewardship last week! But I wonder if we really would be happy if we had all the money we could possibly spend.

Bob: Maybe not. But let's put that thought "on hold" and decide what we're going to do tonight.

Carol: What would you like to do?

Bob: This waterbed looks pretty good. I'd say we ought to try it out!

Carol: I'd say we ought to watch a movie. There are a couple of good ones on TV.

Bob: Well, let's flip a coin. Heads it's the waterbed. Tails it's the movie. (He flips a quarter.) Aha, it's heads! Who said money doesn't talk? See you under the covers. We've never made love on a waterbed!

Carol: Can't we both be winners? I really want to see the movie *It Could Happen to You.*

They both were winners that night.

_____

How did you feel as you read the dialogue between Carol and Bob? Have you ever had discussions like this? When? Where? Can you recall a decision you have made about spending more money on something than you could afford because you thought it would make you happy—but it didn't? Have you talked together about how your parents handled finances? Has their pattern of spending become your own in marriage?

After discussing these questions, take a few minutes to list some of the concerns you have about money and the ways you are spending and saving it. Be honest and open without allowing your conversation to become argumentative. Keep this list with you as you continue making your way through this chapter.

OUR CONCERNS ABOUT MONEY

Take a break now and take out a dollar bill. Place it on this book and look at it for a few minutes. Then remember the first dollar you ever earned—not received as an allowance or gift. How did you earn it? How old were you? How did you spend or save your dollar? If you can't remember exactly, try to remember a time when you felt very happy about having a dollar bill to spend however you wanted. After sharing your memories, take time for a brief devotion before continuing to the next section. If you are unable to continue at this time, plan when you will resume your exploration of this chapter.

Devotional Thought: "Do not store up for yourselves treasures on earth, where moth and rust consume and where thieves break in and steal ... For where your treasure is, there your heart will be also" (Matthew 6:19, 21).

Prayer: Help us, O God, not to allow our finances to harm our relationship in any way. Keep us from being anxious about money and intent on saving so much for the future that we do not enjoy today or share with others. Remind us to give ourselves and the simple things that can bring just as much joy as expensive gifts. " 'Tis a gift to be simple, 'tis a gift to be free."

---

2. Wants Vs. Needs: Practicing Good Stewardship

Let's join Bob and Carol the next morning in the spacious restaurant at the time-share lodge. As they linger over breakfast, they are discussing their wants and needs and how these affect their spending and saving habits.

Bob: How about this buffet, Carol? I've never had so many different things for breakfast in my life! Maybe we could do this every Saturday morning at home.

Carol: Are you asking me to cook all this every Saturday? Dream on, Bob!

Bob: No, No—I mean go out for an all-you-can-eat breakfast. Robbie would love it. I bet at some places three-year-olds eat for half price—or free!

Carol: It looks like we're back to money again. *You* and *I* don't eat free, you know!

Bob: That's why I brought this pad and pencil with me. I got to thinking about what we said last night, and I thought we might try something. Why don't we draw a line down the middle of the paper and list everything we want to purchase on the left side and everything we already own that we don't really need on the right side? Wouldn't that help us with the planning you said we need to do?

Carol: I don't know. What would it do for us? We'd just end up with a "wish list" and a "give away" list.

Bob: It would be more than that. We could put down the approximate cost of each item we want, and then we'd be able to see what we can afford to buy now and what we need to save for. And if we gave an approximate value to everything we have but don't need, we could see how much we'd make if we sold those items—or how much we could claim on our taxes if we gave them away.

Carol: You know, maybe we don't actually need everything we might "want." And how are we going to get any money from the things we *don't want* anymore? Nobody else will want them either.

Bob: Well, after we've listed all the things we want, we could go back and prioritize them. We might write a #1 beside those things that really are needs, a #2 beside those things that would be helpful to have but are not essential, and a #3 beside those things we can live without. That would probably take some time—and a lot of discussion.

Carol: You're right, but that's something we really need to do.

Bob: About the things we don't want or need anymore—you just might be surprised at the money we could make. Remember when Fred and Amy had their garage sale last spring? They actually cleared $275.00!

Carol: I hate garage sales! They're a mess to organize, a mess to clean up, and a mess all the way through! A garage sale would make me feel kind of cheap. I wouldn't want the neighbors to think we were trying to make money that way!

Bob: Lots of people do it, Carol, and lots of people enjoy going to garage sales. If it's not your thing, then how about letting me and Robbie have one? We'll call it "Robbie's Garage Sale." He can sit on a stool right beside the change box, which we'll label "Robbie's College Fund." People will love it!

Carol: Sounds a little silly to me, but if you and Robbie want to do it together, maybe it would be okay. Count on me to be gone that day!

Bob: Well, maybe we won't do it exactly that way, but it's got possibilities. We could even give some of the money we make to the church or another charity.

Carol: It's starting to sound better to me now.

Bob: Besides having a garage sale, we could give some things to the church bazaar and other charities—and we could file a receipt on our 1040. We'd benefit, and so would those who get some of the things they need.

Carol: I like that idea. Since it's your idea to do these lists, why don't you draw the columns while I get some more coffee and one of those Belgian waffles with strawberries and whipped cream!

Bob: It's a deal. Bring me one of those waffles, too, please.

Bob took the pad and drew two columns, adding the headings "Wants/Needs" and "Things Not Needed Anymore." Then he drew a "cost/value" column for each. After making their lists, Bob and Carol discussed each item they had listed in the want/need column, trying to determine how to differentiate between their wants and needs. At first they found it difficult to agree which were *wants* and which were *needs*, realizing as they talked that if either of them had wanted to buy something, it had been considered a need. Now they were seeing more clearly that not all wants are needs.

They soon agreed to go through the list more than once, reviewing those items designated as "real needs" (#1) and "helpful to have, but not essential" (#2) a second and third time so that they might determine if they really *needed* everything they *wanted*. Cost was a primary factor in helping to identify which items they had listed as "needs" were actually "wants." The things they had marked "can live without" (#3) were considered future "if-ever" items and were not the cause of much discussion.

Bob and Carol kept the criteria of cost, comfort, and convenience in focus throughout this process. For example, one critical "need" (#1) they listed was a new washing machine, because their old one was beyond repair. Another item they listed as a "need" (#1) but later changed to a helpful but nonessential "want" (#2) was a CD player, which would replace the old but still functional tape player they currently had. An item they listed as something they could live without (#3) was a bread machine.

As they considered a saving/purchasing plan in relation to their "needs" and "wants," Bob and Carol decided to establish a specific amount of money to set aside each month, depositing the money in a checking/savings account unless it was needed immediately for a critical expenditure. Any needs that required more than this monthly amount—or more than their accumulated savings—they would charge on a credit card, with the agreed stipulation that no other items could be charged until the account had been paid in full. They realized, of course, that in an extreme emergency, they would have to be flexible enough to allow their credit to be extended to meet the need.

As they talked about what items to give away or sell, they suddenly began to share the feeling that "this is good—this is fun." They realized that the things they had been keeping "in case they were ever needed" were simply adding to the clutter of their crowded rooms, and they experienced a sense of relief and satisfaction in knowing that some other person or couple could benefit from these items, whether sold or given away.

The overall result of the time Bob and Carol spent that morning at breakfast was a "new perspective" on deciding what they really needed—the values within their home—along with the realization that their finances could be seen as a challenge, rather than a problem.

Such a perspective connects our lives with the ultimate values we need to establish in marriage and the responsibility of each of us in relation to the world around us. This is known as stewardship. Stewardship defines who we are as individuals and as couples. What we do with what we have received—including not only our money but also our time and talents—is the test that determines whether we are responsible citizens of God's world.

In the story of the prodigal son (Luke 15), Jesus tells how a son wasted his entire inheritance in careless, foolish expenditures. Good stewardship means careful, prayerful decisions about how we use our money and other resources to enhance life and return a portion to God, who has given so much to us directly and indirectly through health and strength, as well as insights and understanding of the richness of the natural world. In addition, stewardship means *investing* our resources in ways that will be productive, as Jesus taught in the parable of the talents (Matthew 25). In this parable, Jesus contrasts the joy of the man who doubled his original investment with the sadness of the man who, because of fear, hid what he could have invested.

Similarly, good stewardship in marriage means investing *all* of life in a way that will be productive, preserve the goodness of creation, and return some of what we have received to the Giver of every good and perfect gift (James 1:12). When a couple is focused on their "wants" and "needs" in a creative understanding of stewardship, the challenge to continually "sort through" things they no longer need prompts them to sell or give away items that may be used and valued by others. In many ways this is "recycling," which is good stewardship. The challenge for most couples is taking the time to do this on a regular basis.

Take time now to work together to complete your own inventory of "wants/needs" and "things not needed anymore" using the following form. After completing your lists and adding the cost or value amount for each item, prioritize those things included in the "wants/needs" column, writing a #1 beside things that really are needs, a #2 beside those that would be helpful to have but are not essential, and a #3 beside those you can live without. Share openly and honestly and listen to each other carefully as you determine what criteria to use. It's likely that each of you will have to make some compromises along the way. What discoveries about similarities and differences in your priorities and views of money does this part of the exercise reveal? What concerns or disagreements require further discussion?

Our Inventory of "Wants/Needs" and "Things Not Needed Anymore"			
"Wants/Needs"	Cost	"Things Not Needed Anymore"	Value

Be sure to recognize conflict for what it is. Conflict about money is not always related to dollar amounts, but often reflects a different set of values, possibly the result of different family backgrounds. Do not allow conflict about money to be destructive in relation to your overall values. Follow these guidelines in order to ensure healthy communication about money: (1) listen carefully to each other, (2) set time limits for discussion; and (3) agree that each of you will respect the viewpoints of the other and seek to compromise as necessary.

Now consider how you might plan to purchase or save for the items labeled #1 and #2 in the months and years ahead. What changes in your spending and saving habits do you think this plan might require?

Finally, take a close look at when and where you could sell or give away items listed in the right-hand column. Are there individuals in your church or community that might be in need of some of these items? Are there other ways you might practice good stewardship of these items, such as giving an old sofa to a homeless shelter or church youth group? What will you do with the money you receive from selling any of these items? In light of this exercise, what changes or adjustments do each of you need to make in order to become good stewards of the resources God has given you?

Take a short break now. Stretch and have a snack, if you like. Just for fun, you might figure out how much your snack might cost if you bought it already made and how much it would cost if you made it yourself! After your break, you will explore budget planning and its importance to your marriage.

3. Financial Planning: A Partnership of Trust

Financial planning is a matter of looking ahead. Just as planning is the key to success in all areas of marriage—whether it be a special meal, a business trip, a vacation, or even a weekly schedule of activities—so financial planning is doing your homework ahead of time so that right decisions will result, like right answers on a test.

Financial planning is a partnership of trust, because not everything can be foreseen. It is trusting each other as you create the best financial plan you can. It is trusting each other, along with God's guidance, to do the very best you can to meet the needs of the present as well as the future. It is trusting—and having increased confidence—that the ideas you share will produce good results and that the money you spend and save will enhance your life together. A partnership of trust is an extension of a covenant of love.

The importance of financial planning to a healthy marriage can be seen in the true-life stories of many couples who reach distant goals and celebrate life along the way. It is good to observe how other couples have made such accomplishments—not all at once, but through a step-by-step process. It also is helpful to enlist the counsel of a financial planner and/or attend a seminar sponsored by your church or another organization.

Basic to your financial plan is the creation of a monthly budget. The success of this monthly budget will depend upon your ability to be realistic about available resources. Once you have created a monthly budget, you are ready to develop an overall financial plan that projects income for one month at a time, allocating a portion to be saved for the future needs that are part of your long-range goals.

This chapter is not intended to tell you all you need to know about financial planning or the detailed and intricate process of creating a monthly budget. There are many excellent books to help you, some of which are listed in the bibliography. Our purpose is to help you think and talk together about how you currently spend and save money and consider what changes, if any, you may need to make.

In order to do this, look at the process as something you can approach creatively together—right now. Identifying areas where you may be spending too much or too little is a helpful first step in creating or revising a monthly budget. Agree to participate in the following budget exercise with an open mind and a fresh outlook on the ways you spend your money.

Get some change from a purse or dresser drawer in the following amounts: two dimes, eight nickels, and forty pennies. Place the coins on a small table, along with a blank sheet of paper and pencil. A calculator also might be handy to have on hand.

First, write on the paper every monthly "expense" you can think of, including money allocated for church, charities, and savings (see the following sample worksheet). Then discuss how you would allocate the change to cover all your *current* monthly expenses if one dollar represented your total monthly income. In other words, determine how many pennies, nickels, or dimes would represent the percentage of total monthly income you spend *on average* in each category. For example, in the sample worksheet you probably will consider rent/mortgage a major item that requires a much higher percentage of your total monthly income than household supplies or recreation/entertainment. Therefore, it would be good to cover the major fixed items first and then proceed with allocating available pennies or nickels to categories that are more flexible. Note: If you do not know what your current average monthly expenses are in one or more categories, then that is an important first step. Without that information, you cannot begin to think about creating or revising a budget.

Let this exercise be something of a game. Take turns moving the coins around as you think they should be divided. Try to reach an agreement about how your income is divided, coming as close as you can to the actual percentage of total monthly income you spend in every item or category. Do not allow this to become a "win-lose" game; rather, think of it as a creative look at how you are managing your finances.

When you reach agreement, play the game again, this time placing the coins not according to how your monthly income is allocated now, but according to how you think it *should be* allocated. Of course, this will be more difficult, especially if you have differing views about how your money should be spent or saved. As you did in the previous exercise, share openly and honestly and listen to each other carefully. What discoveries about similarities and differences in your priorities and your views of money does this part of the exercise reveal? What concerns or disagreements require further discussion? What changes in your spending or saving habits, if any, will you agree to make? Remember that any changes will require looking carefully at what you want to do and whether you have the resources.

Sample Worksheet

Rent/Mortgage	Transportation	Medical/Dental (& Prescriptions)
Food	Recreation/ Entertainment	Insurance
Clothing	Education/Day Care	Household Supplies
Utilities	Savings/Investments	Subscriptions
Charity (church and others)	Gifts, Cards, Postage	Other:

If you are like most couples, you probably have identified one or more areas where you need to modify your spending patterns. In our materialistic society, most of us would benefit from simplifying our lifestyles and reducing our expenses and debt. In her book *Simplify Your Life* (New York: Hyperion, 1994, pp. 99-124), Elaine St. James identifies a number of ways to save money through simple steps that require planning, determination, and discipline. As you look at the following summary of some of her suggestions, each of you check the three ideas you think would be most helpful to explore further.

1. Take steps to get out of debt. Sit down and figure out exactly how much you owe; then work out a plan to pay it off as quickly and methodically as possible.
2. Live on less than you earn. Living simply is not a matter of living cheaply or of feeling deprived. It's an opportunity to get in touch with what is really important in your life.
3. Designate one day a week for shopping. This day should include groceries and everything else you need for the week.
4. Delay all major purchases, and even some minor ones, for at least two weeks to one month. This will help you decide whether you really need an item.
5. Try to come up with a creative solution, rather than a "buying solution" to whatever need you have. (For example, instead of buying hand-held weights for use when walking or exercising, try using socks filled with sand or other household items.)
6. When you feel you need to go shopping just to see what you can find, leave your cash, checkbook, and credit cards at home.
7. Pay for most everything you buy with checks. This may be more difficult than paying with cash or a bank draft card, but it is an easier way to keep track of what you buy and how you spend your money.
8. Get rid of all credit cards except one. Pay off the balance each month to avoid any interest and service charge.
9. Next time you're in the market for a car, buy one secondhand, and if possible, buy directly from the owner. (A new car loses 30 percent of its value the moment you drive it off the sales lot.)
10. Teach your children fiscal responsibility. Encourage them to save half of what they earn from allowances or part-time jobs. Teaching your children how to handle their money is one of the most powerful gifts you can give them.

Other good resources to consult for ideas related to improving your finances include those listed in the bibliography and perhaps those related to stewardship in your church library. Remember, your future financial picture depends on how you plan *now*. Sound financial planning is the key to maintaining an ongoing sense of security within your marriage. It relates not only to money in terms of purchasing power, but also to preserving values, enhancing family life, and sharing with those who are part of our global family.

Pause now for a brief devotion before moving on to the final section of this chapter.

Devotional Thought: "For which of you, intending to build a tower, does not first sit down and estimate the cost, to see whether he has enough to complete it?" (Luke 14:28)

Prayer: Help us, O God, to know how and when to spend the money we have and how and when to save for the future; help us to keep our priorities in order by keeping us aware of what is most important in your sight, so that we do not foolishly waste resources or miss the joy of sharing what we have with others. Amen.

---

5. The Joy of Giving

One of the most important lessons we can learn is that the inner life—the soul—is enriched through the act of giving. The world, however, seems to be focused on "what we get" rather than "what we give." Harry Emerson Fosdick's beautiful hymn "God of Grace and God of Glory" warns us that we may be "rich in things and poor in soul." Think about *how you feel inside* when you give something to others, rather than keeping everything for yourself. What word would you use to describe this feeling?

As we've often said, "The joy of living stems from the joy of giving." Giving some of what you have to others is one of the greatest sources of joy you can experience, and you don't need to be rich to experience this joy. In fact, it has nothing to do with the amount of money you have in the bank or the size of your paycheck. Many couples discover this for themselves early in marriage. Some, however, wait far too long to give of their resources, thinking they do not have enough money. But the truth is that you can give even a very small amount and experience great joy because of your motivation to give. Giving whatever you can to meet a need brings a sense of happiness and fulfillment that is hard to describe.

There are unlimited ways you can give to others. One of the best is to give to your church. The church, in particular, is a place where we, as people of faith who understand God's goodness to us, can share with those who are less fortunate. In fact, it was through the church that early believers learned this truth: "It is more blessed to give than to receive" (Acts 20:35). Deciding how much you will give to your church should be a decision you reach together.

Many couples follow the biblical model of tithing, set a goal to give 10 percent of their household income to support the needs and ministries of the church, even though they may have limited income. In the third chapter of Malachi, we find this promise: "Bring the full tithe into the storehouse . . . and thus put me to the test, says the LORD of hosts; see if I will not open the windows of heaven for you and pour down for you an overflowing blessing" (v. 10). If you are unable to give this much right now, perhaps you can start at a lower percentage and gradually increase your giving to 10 percent—or more. You will find that, perhaps more than anything else you might do, this one act of giving will bring immeasurable joy to your lives.

Although giving to the church is one of the most effective ways to channel your financial gifts to those in need, you also may want to make donations to worthy charitable organizations. Many couples consider gifts to charitable organizations part of their tithe or whatever percentage they are able to give to "do God's work" here on earth. There are many ways in which such organizations provide help for needy families, especially children, in our own country and throughout the world. Unfortunately, today we are bombarded with so many solicitations—many through telemarketing—from all kinds of causes that sound worthy that we have difficulty determining which ones to support. One of the criteria you should use is to give only to those organizations that explain fully how the money will be allocated, including how much will be used for overhead or office management of funds. Sometimes solicitors sound very compassionate and seem to be sincere about meeting human needs, yet a large percentage of the money is used for other purposes. It also may be helpful to discuss various charities or appeals with your pastor, a group or class at your church, or other friends, to determine which are more deserving of support. Remember, above all, that the purpose of giving to others is to share genuinely in meeting needs, for all of us are members of the human family.

Of course, there are many other ways to help meet the needs of others, such as giving to coworkers and persons in your neighborhood or community who have experienced tragedies of loss, are undergoing a serious health crisis, or are caring for others with disabilities. Children are always an important and special focus. Be alert and aware of children who are homeless or need extra care and love.

Again, remember that giving does not always have to be monetary. We can give of our time and talents by tutoring, providing transportation or meals, washing clothes, cleaning house, cutting grass, and many other personal efforts of caring and sharing. There also are many opportunities beyond the local community, such as serving on mission teams sent to disaster areas to help communities rebuild after floods and other natural disasters.

Take a few minutes now to discuss ways you can give some of what you have to others—whether your gift be money, possessions, time, or something else—completing the following chart as you talk. Wherever applicable, include the specific dollar amount and percentage of your income that you will give—or that is part of your current giving pattern. Let this be an open-ended process as you consider how you can experience the joy of giving.

Ways We Can Experience the Joy of Giving

Organizations or Individuals	Dollar Amount or Description of Gift	% of Income (if $ amount)	When?
Our Church:			
Other Charitable Organizations:			
Individuals:			
Other:			

Devotional Thought: "Each of you must give . . . not reluctantly or under compulsion, for God loves a cheerful giver" (2 Corinthians 9:7).

Prayer: We thank you, God, for the good gifts you have given us—even when we think that we do not have enough or that others have received more than they deserve. Help us to commit ourselves to giving what we can to others, and to do so with cheerfulness, so that we may know the joy of giving. Amen.

"For richer or poorer." This is the commitment you have made to each other. In order to keep it, you must view yourselves as "financial partners" who are committed to openly discussing all issues related to this important area of your marriage, working together to find creative solutions to challenges and setbacks. Refer again to the concerns you listed. Are there any that you have not covered, or that require additional exploration and/or discussion? Where can you turn for guidance or assistance? What plans can you make now to address some of these issues together?

Remember that even when you find yourselves in financial crisis, there is hope. Investigate every possibility of help—such as consulting financial counselors, restructuring budget, delaying purchases, or deciding to "go for it" in terms of implementing a solution. Never let money problems keep the two of you from sharing your love—the greatest resource you can give or receive.

Most important, remember that God's love is unlimited. It is what makes you truly rich, regardless of what you may or may not have in the bank! Continually remind yourself of the blessings God has given you.

7. IN SICKNESS AND IN HEALTH

▼

When saying your wedding vows, you promised to love each other "in sickness and in health," as long as you both shall live. The commitment to love when both of you are healthy is simple. What about when one of you is sick with the flu or another minor illness? Do you complain a lot? Does your partner understand that? Do you need a great deal of tender loving care? Is one of you more nurturing at such times? Couples rarely take the time to think or discuss such questions; instead, they make it through times of illness case by case, giving little thought to their needs, expectations, or ways of interacting during such times.

One woman in her seventies and eighties used to say, "If I die . . .". As she approaches her ninetieth birthday, she now says, "When I die . . .". Of course, we know that we all will die. But have you ever thought about what you will do if one of you should have a major health problem or a chronic or terminal illness? It is very likely that this will happen sometime during your life together. In some cases, unfortunately, it is sooner rather than later. How you think and talk about it now can help you to be better prepared.

Sadly, sometimes persons are unable to handle difficult health situations involving their mates. A young husband could not bear to see his lovely young bride dying from cancer; he left her. A wife was in her forties when her husband became ill. As much as she wanted to, she could not go to the hospital to see him; she couldn't bear to think of being alone or of their children being without their father. A husband died suddenly of a heart attack; he and his wife had never talked about such a possibility. She was unprepared emotionally, spiritually, and financially for such a tragedy. It is difficult even to think about these kinds of situations, much less talk about them—particularly in the early years of marriage—but it is extremely important to discuss such possibilities *before* they happen.

This chapter will help you to think about and discuss everyday health issues, as well as major health concerns—both of which significantly affect your marriage relationship. If you are both in good health now, thank God! Then ask yourselves, how can we stay that way? If one or both of you currently are not in good health, ask God to bring healing and wholeness into your life. Then ask yourselves what you can do to assist in this process.

Go to the medicine cabinet now and get a Band-Aid or some other first-aid item. As you reflect together on the times in your marriage when one or both of you have had specific health needs, let this item be a visual symbol or focus, reminding you of how you treated the particular need.

1. Taking Inventory of Our Health Needs

Today we are more conscious of preventive health care, emphasizing the importance of exercising and eating a balanced diet—including a preoccupation with monitoring fat grams and weight gain to control blood pressure, avoid high cholesterol, and possibly prevent heart attacks and other health problems. Although this focus on health can be *un*healthy when unrealistic images of thin models and perfect bodies are our motivation, considering our health needs as married couples can help us keep the commitment we made to love each other "in sickness and in health."

Sometimes one partner may complain to the other, "I just don't have the energy I used to have," or "I'd really like to get back in shape, but I don't have time." Charting your "health record" can help you anticipate and prepare for the future with a positive outlook. It also allows you to see when and why you were feeling better than at other times. In addition to this exercise, you can take an inventory of your own needs simply by asking each other questions similar to those on an intake sheet in a physician's office.

The following example shows how one couple plotted their "health record" during the six years of their marriage. The solid line represents the wife's health and the dotted line represents the husband's health. As you look at their graph, note that they considered their times of poor health to be when an accident occurred or when they were diagnosed with a specific illness. These incidents had more of a long-term effect than one might expect. In contrast, they experienced times of good health when they had made intentional efforts to bring about a change through exercises, diet, or vacations. Physical health, then, is always relative to our emotional outlook, which accompanies both extremes.

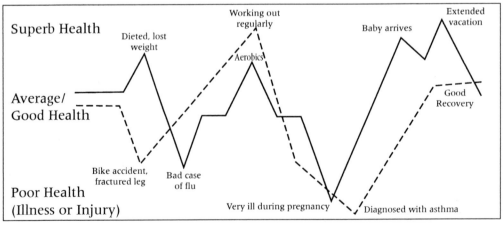

Chart your own "health record" by creating a graph in the space provided. At the bottom, number the months or years you have been married from left to right. Then corresponding with the years of your marriage, plot times of illness or poor health in the lower half and times of good to superb health in the upper half. Now connect the dots. Use different colors of pencils or pens to distinguish your lines.

Our Health Record

Superb Health

Average/
Good Health

Poor Health
(Illness or Injury)

As you discuss the times of poor health and good health that each of you plotted on the chart, try to remember how you felt at each of those times about yourself and/or about the way your spouse may have responded to your attempts to be helpful or provide care. Talk openly about the following questions: What worries, if any, did you have during times of poor health or serious illness? Did you express your feelings to your partner? To a doctor? To other family members or friends? Did you pray for healing? How did you help each other through those times? How did you feel during those times when one or both of you had good or excellent health? What specific health needs have you had in the past that you might anticipate having again? What changes in your previous responses to these needs would you make in the future? What other observations can you make about your "health record" and any possible implications it may have for your future?

An intentional wellness program can help you and your partner improve not only your health record but also your relationship. When you have a loving, caring concern for the well-being of each other, there is a supportive emotional effect that gives a new sense of hope, a feeling of self-worth, and an appreciation for each other that is quite different from the critical, complaining syndrome that typifies some marriages. As you share in physical exercise and other activities that promote good health, you will progress toward goals that help you become the persons God intends you to be.

Any goals that move you toward well-being should be high priorities, because pursuing these goals will help you to experience health and wholeness in every area of your lives. Even if you should have critical health problems or serious physical limitations, efforts to improve your state of well-being—ever so gradually—can provide hope and give you a healthy outlook on life.

2. Working Toward Health and Wholeness

As creations of God, our health involves the physical, mental/emotional, and spiritual aspects of our lives. In the Bible we find instructions and promises related to each of these. As you work toward wholeness through physical, mental/emotional, and spiritual health, you might find it helpful to memorize a few of these verses. Here are a few to start with:

Physical: "For we are the temple of the living God." (2 Corinthians 6:16*b*)

Mental: "Do not let your hearts be troubled." (John 14:1)

Emotional: "Be transformed by the renewing of your minds, so that you may discern what is the will of God." (Romans 12:2*b*)

Spiritual: "Pray then in this way:
Our Father in heaven . . ." (see Matthew 6:9-13)
"Trust in the LORD with all your heart,
and do not rely on your own insight.
In all your ways acknowledge him,
and he will make straight your paths." (Proverbs 3:5-6)

Remember that God intends us to be healthy and whole, as you look together now at your physical, mental, and spiritual health.

Physical Health: Designing a Wellness Program

You have already discussed some of your health needs. The following checklist will help you identify specific needs related to your physical health, as well as affirm some of the positive steps you currently are taking toward health and wholeness.

Take turns responding to the following statements, covering over the answers of your partner as necessary.

Habits for Physical Health

As a responsible partner in marriage, I do the following:

YES	NO		YES	NO
___	___	Have an annual physical exam.	___	___
___	___	Try to eat a balanced diet, avoiding excesses.	___	___
___	___	Get some kind of exercise on a regular basis.	___	___
___	___	Pursue a specific exercise program (e.g., participating in an aerobics class, swimming, working out at the gym).	___	___
___	___	Take vitamins and other dietary supplements and/ or prescription medications as directed by physicians.	___	___
___	___	Get adequate sleep each night.	___	___
___	___	Schedule specific precautionary exams (e.g., mammogram, prostate exam, etc.).	___	___
___	___	Avoid excessive consumption of caffeine.	___	___
___	___	Follow a general practice of personal hygiene, which enhances overall health.	___	___
___	___	Take time to relax in order to reduce tension, which can cause physical and emotional illnesses.	___	___
___	___	Talk openly with my spouse about health concerns.	___	___

Others:

As you look at your answers together, focus specifically on the "no" responses. Discuss how and when you could take steps to improve in these areas—either individually or together. Do not allow yourselves to be critical of each other with "I told you so" responses. Rather, try to be open and helpful, realizing that it is impossible to accomplish everything at once. Instead, you must begin with those things that seem to be of greatest importance or cause for most concern. Be careful not to over-monitor your bodily health. Follow up periodically by sharing "progress reports" and identifying other items that need attention. This can be a challenging experience that leads to better health and longer life.

Remember that goals must be reviewed and sometimes revised, even though they may seem so easy to attain at first. To keep your goals realistic, it is important to prioritize as you go along. In some instances, you may need to give yourselves more time to achieve certain goals; in other cases you may need to modify your goals, such as choosing a different schedule for exercise than you first planned.

What if one of you is reluctant to participate in an effort to improve physical health or refuses to practice good health habits? Sometimes the support of a physician can be very helpful, if the doctor uses a caring rather than a critical approach. Other times, it may be helpful to agree on minimal objectives at first, encouraging each other to make whatever progress you can without comparing yourselves.

You can avoid unnecessary conflict by complimenting each other on any progress and by sharing serious disagreements about your goals with an objective third party "advisor" or counselor. Encouragement and motivation are the secrets to success, even in the midst of setbacks. Remember, however, you cannot be responsible for your partner's health. Responses such as, "I understand," "I'll help if I can," or "I care so much for you" can help dissolve feelings of resentment and frustration. Laughter is also one of the best ways to relieve tension when talking about health—that is, laughing *with* each other, not *at* each other.

Remember, of course, that you cannot achieve the goal of good health if you abuse your physical or mental capabilities in any way. Often individuals are guilty of abusing themselves without even realizing it. The addictive behavior might be dieting, overeating, using tobacco or alcohol or other drugs, or overworking themselves. Even the subtle addiction of workaholism can produce consequences as serious as those caused by alcoholism, though the effects on family members may differ.

The first step in overcoming addictive behavior is to acknowledge it. Therefore, it is particularly important that you look carefully at your lifestyle and consider any patterns that might lead to a possible addiction for either of you. If addressed early enough, almost every destructive behavior can be changed and replaced with another habit or "focus" that leads to wholeness and well-being—both physically and mentally. A physician is essential to this process; a counselor or therapist with special expertise often can be of tremendous help as well. Never neglect the opportunity for healing and wholeness. After all, it benefits not one but both of you, for when one partner is hurting in any way, so is the other—at least this is true in marriages where love forms the circle.

Mental and Emotional Health: Developing a Healthy Outlook

In the Bible we read, "A merry heart is good medicine" (Proverbs 17:22). How true! As Norman Cousins proved by his own experience, laughter facilitates healing. After being diagnosed with an unknown terminal illness,

Cousins began watching humorous videos and laughing as much as possible. He later wrote a book about his experience of healing and the benefits of humor in the healing process.

Like laughter, a positive outlook also helps both body and mind. Norman Vincent Peale devoted his life to helping people cultivate the "power of positive thinking," which has changed the lives of countless people in many different ways—from physical healing to relational healing to spiritual healing. The psychological term, *cognitive therapy*, is used to describe this process of helping people change wrong attitudes or thought patterns into positive ones.

In her book *Don't Put a Period Where God Put a Comma*, Nell Mohney describes certain attitudes that we should cultivate in order to become more positive, optimistic people, including gratitude, magnanimity, and compassion (Nashville: Dimensions for Living, 1993, 57-60). *Gratitude*, she says seems to open "your heart to life, to others, and to God." Ask yourself, How often do I say "thank you" to my spouse? Do I thank others? *Magnanimity*, according to Mohney, is "being generous instead of petty. You need to see every person as a child of God, a person of worth, even if you don't agree with or like him or her." Do you accept others for *who* they are, regardless of *what* they may say or do? Finally, she defines *compassion* as "the ability to feel with others." Rather than worry for others, we should *feel with them* or empathize with them. Empathy is a helpful way of thinking about what it means to have compassion. Can you recognize and understand why some people are critical, sad, or upset by experiences or circumstances they are going through?

What is your E. H. Q. (Emotional Health Quotient)? Find out by taking the following E. H. Q. inventory. Make a copy of the inventory if possible, or mark your answers in your notebooks.

My E. H. Q. Inventory

1. I begin each day with a positive attitude. "This is the day that the Lord has made; [I will] rejoice and be glad in it" (Psalm 118:24).

___ usually   ___ sometimes   ___ once in a while   ___ not very often

2. I try to change my negative thoughts to "I can do this" or "I will be able to get through this," remembering, "I can do all things through [Christ] who strengthens me" (Philippians 4:13).

___ usually   ___ sometimes   ___ once in a while   ___ not very often

3. I try to check my critical attitudes toward people, trying not to blame others or talk unkindly about them, even if what I say may be true.

___ usually   ___ sometimes   ___ once in a while   ___ not very often

4. I smile at my spouse, children, and others.

___ usually   ___ sometimes   ___ once in a while   ___ not very often

---

5. I realize that it's only when I *accept* unfair blame or criticism that it can hurt me.

___ usually ___ sometimes ___ once in a while ___ not very often

6. Rather than letting anger build up within me or thinking about it a lot, I can let it go or talk to someone—in the right way—if something is really bothering me.

___ usually ___ sometimes ___ once in a while ___ not very often

7. I truly try to accept each person; if I dislike someone's undesirable traits or wrong acts, I try to understand, hating the act rather than the person.

___ usually ___ sometimes ___ once in a while ___ not very often

8. I try not to have unrealistic expectations. Instead of expecting others to be perfect, I try to have faith in them and enjoy them.

___ usually ___ sometimes ___ once in a while ___ not very often

9. I try to love the unlovable; they are the ones who most need love. I remind myself that everyone needs someone to love him or her, remembering the promise, "I will show you a still more excellent way" (1 Corinthians 12:31).

___ usually ___ sometimes ___ once in a while ___ not very often

10. I have a positive image of the person I want to be—patient, kind, loving, and generous—and I try to act this way, with God's help. I consider someone who possesses these characteristics not as someone to envy, but as a role model.

___ usually ___ sometimes ___ once in a while ___ not very often

As we have seen, a positive attitude affects both physical and emotional health. It can help those who are experiencing poor health, pain, and even debilitating illnesses or disabilities to be healthy and "whole" mentally and emotionally.

There are many inspiring examples of persons who have faced physical tragedies with courage and determination, overcoming feelings of despair and self-pity. Perhaps one of the most inspirational examples in recent years is Christopher Reeve, who was thrown from his horse on Memorial Day in 1995, suffering a paralyzing injury to the area between his neck and brain stem. The routines of his daily life as a brilliant actor and loving husband and father suddenly stopped.

In an interview one year after the accident, Reeve shared how his outlook on life had changed from despair to determination:

All that self-pity comes in the beginning. And it does recur. But what you begin to say to yourself instead of "What life do I have?" is "What life can I build?" And the answer, surprisingly, is "More than you think." ("New Hopes, New Dreams," *Time* 148, no. 10 [August 26, 1996]: 40-52)

As a result of his positive attitude, Reeve decided to take action to help not only his own cause but that of all the other paraplegics by launching a one-man publicity and lobbying campaign that has had incredible results.

Although we may not be well-known personalities and our medical crises may not be as extreme, all of us can cultivate a positive attitude and surround one another with tenderness and encouragement. Prayer is an essential tool that we can use to make this happen.

Spiritual Health: Exploring the Power of Prayer

Prayer is not only essential for cultivating a positive outlook on life and finding hope and strength for difficult times, it also has tremendous power to bring health and healing.

If someone is looking for Dr. Ben Carson, world-renowned neurological surgeon at Johns Hopkins Hospital—one of at least five major schools that offer a program in spirituality and healing, nurses often respond to the person inquiring, "He's praying before he operates." Likewise, besides prescribing medicine for his patients, Dr. Dale Matthews, associate professor of medicine at Georgetown University Medical Center, *prays with them.* Interestingly, he has found that after praying with a patient, the patient's blood pressure immediately drops (*Christianity Today,* January 6, 1997). According to Dr. Larry Dossey, "One of the best kept secrets in modern medicine is prayer" ("Can Prayer Heal?" *Today's Health* 16 [April 1994]: 22).

Increasingly, research findings from the medical community support the healing power of prayer and religious belief. In a survey conducted by Yankelovich Partners at the American Academy of Family Physicians, 99 of 296 doctors believe that religious belief can bring healing. Seventy-five percent of the doctors surveyed also believe prayers of others can facilitate a patient's recovery (*Jet* [December 23, 1996], Johnson Publishing Company). Another study conducted in 1994 by Wayne State University showed that persons who regularly attend church suffer depression less often and generally have healthier lifestyles.

Duke University psychiatrist Harold Koenig, who has studied the general and specific health benefits of religion and faith, also supports the claim that "church-related activity may prevent illness." His studies have indicated that those who watch religious television and pray at home do not enjoy the same health benefits as those who participate in religious services outside the home, signaling the importance of community to spiritual health and healing (*Christianity Today* [January 6, 1997]: 22-23).

There is no question that prayer and spiritual connectedness *can* help in the healing of physical, emotional, and mental problems. Although prayers for healing are not a substitute for medical help, they are an important part of the total process of healing. There are many reports of miraculous healing coming through the prayers of individuals and groups, as well as through services conducted by "faith healers." It is important to recognize, however, that miracles occur in many different ways, and that even when there is no immediate physical healing, God's love continues to surround those who pray for health and wholeness, providing an "inner healing" and spiritual vitality beyond what they could experience otherwise.

When prayers for physical healing go unanswered, people sometimes question whether those doing the praying have enough faith in God. This doubt can lead to a sense of guilt and unworthiness. Yet prayers for the health of others are never without answers from God, who provides the courage, patience, and "peace within" that make all the difference to those who are facing pain and uncertainty about the future. Prayer also brings comfort, confidence, and hope to all involved—those who are ill as well as concerned loved ones and friends. It is important to remember that through prayer, God can heal the soul and spirit when physical healing may not be possible.

As you continue to think about your health needs as partners in marriage, remember that it is God's plan for you to be as healthy as possible. Prayer, then, is essential to your marriage. Praying to God for healing and strength *for yourselves* is as important as praying for the needs of others; after all, when you are in good health, you are better able to care for each other and help meet the needs of those around you. In the book of James we find this guideline: "Are any among you suffering? They should pray. Are any cheerful? They should sing songs of praise" (5:13).

Just as Jesus prayed for the protection of his disciples in John 17, so also you are to pray for each other. As you make "ongoing prayers" for each other a part of your daily life, you will become conscious of God being with you all the time. In addition to this continuing awareness, you will need to set specific times for focused prayers—times for praying alone and together. You might, for example, take time for prayer at the beginning of each day, placing the physical, mental/emotional, and spiritual needs of each other and of other family members in God's care and asking for his blessings. Speak of these needs openly during your prayer time, and remember always to thank God when your prayers are answered.

Here are some specific ways you can expand your prayer life as individuals and as a couple:

1. Schedule at least one time each day when you will pray for each other or, preferably, *with* each other. Finding time to pray together is not easy, but it works wonders. If you cannot pray together "in person," choose a specific time when you will pray for health and strength for each other—perhaps

at the beginning of a certain hour of the day—so that each of you will be aware of the other's prayers.

2. Do not be afraid to pray aloud when you are together. As you hear each other "voicing" prayers, remember that God also hears. Let your spoken prayers be a conversation with God, similar to your conversations with each other. Do not be anxious about the words you say; prayer is not a speech contest!

3. Keep a written record of special prayer requests, listing the date and the specific prayer concern. Later on, record when and how each prayer was answered.

4. Write some of your personal prayers for each other in brief paragraphs and post them on the refrigerator or another central place, so that they will continue to remind both of you of your source of help and healing. Remember that your prayers will not be entered in any literary contest; rather, they should be simple letters to God.

5. Pray with others in your home, such as children or close friends who may be present. Ask special blessings for those in the family—near or far—who are in need of healing and hope.

In addition to praying together, try sharing other forms of spiritual nurture, such as singing, studying Bible passages, or sharing devotions on an agreed upon theme or topic. Remember, if you are to maintain health and wholeness as married partners, it is essential that you develop a spiritual life *together.*

Devotional Thought: "Do you not know that you are God's temple and that God's Spirit dwells in you?" (1 Corinthians 3:16); "Those who are well have no need of a physician, but those who are sick" (Matthew 9:12).

Prayer: Help us, O God, to respect our bodies as dwelling places for your Spirit and to care for ourselves and each other in ways that will provide health and strength for daily tasks. May we achieve the goal of health and wholeness by always seeking the help we need from each other, from medical personnel, and most important, from you. Amen.

---

3. Facing Times of Crisis or Serious Illness

Pam and Dave have been married for eighteen months. All is going well. Their priorities, schedules, finances, and overall communication seem to provide a good balance and point toward a great future together.

It is Friday afternoon. Pam and Dave are planning to leave town at 3:15 P.M. to participate in the wedding festivities of Pam's closest friend. In fact, Pam is to be the matron of honor. The rehearsal is at 6:30 P.M., with a dinner following. The drive will take them about two hours, so they should make it in good time. Pam is at home, after leaving her job at noon to make final preparations, and Dave will be arriving any minute.

Their luggage is packed, Pam's dress is hanging neatly in a plastic bag, and the wedding gift is beautifully wrapped. *Where could Dave be?* Pam wonders. *Perhaps he had to work later than he thought he would.* Pam is getting slightly irritated. *Why doesn't he at least call?* She is just about to call Dave's office when the phone rings. *That must be Dave on his car phone, calling to let me know he's on the way.*

She picks up the phone with a sigh of relief, but the voice at the other end of the line is not Dave's.

"Mrs. Harrison, this is the emergency room at Midtown General," the voice says.

Pam gasps and reaches for a chair.

The voice continues, "Your husband, David, has been in an automobile accident. He is just coming back from X ray and is conscious now. He asked that we call you right away."

Pam can't speak for a moment; the phone wavers in her trembling hand. She asks for directions to Midtown General; she's never been there. Then, in a quivering voice, she says, "Tell him that I l-ove h-im, and I'-ll be there soon."

She leaves immediately, whispering a little prayer as she drives: "O God, please help him to live. I need him. I love him. Please, God. . . ."

All thoughts of the wedding fade completely as she makes her way through traffic to the hospital. It is a sunny afternoon, but everything seems to blur as tears well up in her eyes, making it hard to read the sign pointing to the emergency room entrance.

After running through the glass doorway, she breathlessly asks for Dave. A nurse guides her to one of the curtained-off areas, telling her that he is fully conscious now, although heavily sedated.

There is Dave, his lips forming a small smile. "Hi, honey," he almost whispers. A large white bandage circles his head; another covers most of the left side of his face. More bandages are wrapped around his left arm and hand. His left leg is taped to a splint.

"Oh, Dave, I love you so," Pam says. "What happened?"

"I was hit broadside in an intersection by a truck. The car is totaled."

"I don't care about the car. I only care about you. I love you." Then Pam leans over and whispers in his ear, "Don't ever leave me, Dave." Her tears fall on his pillow.

Dave reaches out with the fingers of his right hand to caress her face. His touch suddenly connects them, reminding them that they are one—even in the midst of all the uncertainty.

A doctor pushes back the curtain and comes closer, speaking to Pam: "Your husband is a very lucky man. At first, the medics weren't sure how to get him out of the car. Everything around him was crushed, pinning him inside. He has sustained head injuries, lost a considerable amount of blood, and fractured several bones in his arm and leg. We do not believe there is any damage to his brain, now that he has regained consciousness, but we need to do an MRI to be sure there's no concussion."

"What will happen next?" Pam asks.

"He will need orthopedic surgery to reconstruct the bones in his arm and leg. Some of them are badly shattered," the doctor answers.

"When?"

"We'll be taking him into the OR in just a few minutes, but he wanted to see you first," explains the doctor.

"I'm sorry I can't be with you at the wedding rehearsal," Dave says as the nurse comes to wheel his bed down the hall.

"I'm not going to the wedding, Dave," Pam tells him. "I'm not even thinking about it. I'm only thinking about you."

"But I'm spoiling the whole weekend . . . Ginny and Joe's wedding . . . and what it means to you. You love weddings. Why did this have to happen?"

"But Dave, we still have each other. And that's the most important thing. Isn't that what it's all about? That's why I'm here."

Pam holds his hand tightly as she walks alongside him as far as she can. Then she kisses him gently as he waves good-bye.

———————————

Take a few minutes now to talk together about these questions:

1. How would you feel if this were happening to you? Or if one or both of you have had a serious accident since you've been together, how did you feel? What did you do?
2. If you were Dave, what do you think you might have said to Pam before going into the operating room?
3. If you were Pam, whom would you call after leaving Dave at the operating room doorway? What would you do about the wedding rehearsal and the wedding the next day?
4. Have you or a member of your family ever been in a serious accident or had a serious illness? What was your greatest fear? If you were a child at the time, how did you express your fear—or did you talk about it at all?
5. Do either of you worry that you will lose the other someday because of a serious illness or accident? Are you willing to discuss this openly, or are you afraid to talk about it?

Usually we are not prepared for the crises that disrupt our lives, such as accidents or long-term illnesses. Fortunately, we do not experience these as often as we experience the little discomforts and minor illnesses that affect us for shorter periods and give us less cause for worry. When crises do occur, however, we need to confront them immediately and make necessary adjustments in our lives. That is what Pam and Dave must do, now that their plans for the immediate future have been abruptly interrupted.

A close friend came to be with Pam while Dave was in surgery, and their pastor visited as well. Now it is Saturday morning. Pam has been sleeping in a recliner beside Dave's bed. The sun is streaming through the window, and Pam opens her eyes. She looks over at Dave, who is hooked up to an IV and has casts on his arm and leg. He has been awake for some time. As she reaches for his hand, Pam feels so much hope and gratitude.

Read the following conversation between Pam and Dave aloud, as if you are sharing what they are experiencing.

Dave: Hi, honey. I hope you got some sleep.

Pam: I did—especially the last couple of hours. What about you?

Dave: Yeah, but not all night. I've got this little button I press for more pain medication, and then I feel fine for a while. Right now I don't hurt much at all. In fact, the nurse is bringing me breakfast in a few minutes. Do you want to share it with me?

Pam: I'm not hungry. I'm just so thankful you're still with me. I've been praying that you'll be all right. You were a long time in surgery.

Dave: Well, at least I didn't know what was happening. It sounds like it's going to be a long time until I will be myself again.

Pam: I don't care—just so you can walk again and use your arm and hand, even if it takes a lot of therapy. I'll be there to help you, honey.

Dave: I know you will . . . and the one thing you can do today is go to the wedding. I really want you to be there.

Pam: But Dave, I can't go to a wedding with you in the hospital after a terrible accident.

Dave: Ginny and Joe are counting on you being there, and it would mean so much to them. While you were sleeping, I wrote a little note to the nurse with my good hand. I didn't want to wake you. I asked her if I was going to be Okay today, because I want my wife to go to the wedding of some close friends. She wrote back, "No problem. You're in good hands."

Pam: But what will people think if I'm there having a good time and you're here hurting?

Dave: Wouldn't you want me to do the same thing if you were the one in this bed?

Pam: I guess so, but I'm your *wife*. I want to take care of you, especially at a time like this.

Dave: Don't you think I'd want to take care of you, too? One of the ways you can help me is to keep on going with the rest of life and tell me about it, so I feel as if I'm there, too.

Pam: I don't feel right about it yet—going to the wedding, I mean.

Dave: I think you'll really regret it later if you don't go, Pam. It's only two hours away. Traffic should be light on Saturday. The wedding isn't until 4:00. If you leave at noon, you'll make it in plenty of time, and you can still be back here tonight—or stay over, if you want.

Pam: I wouldn't think of staying overnight, and I'm still not sure about leaving you. Do you *really* think I should go?

Dave: I really do. I'll be okay. Later on we'd both regret it if you didn't go. Just be sure to tell the photographer to take lots of pictures, especially with *you* in them. And bring me a piece of wedding cake.

Pam: But what if something happens to you while I'm gone?

Do-It-Yourself Marriage Enrichment

Dave: Nothing will happen. It's not like I've had heart surgery or serious head injuries. I'll be fine. I'll just keep pressing this little button when I have pain.

Pam: I guess I could make it. Everything is packed at home. I had just put the wedding out of my mind—completely. I'll call Ginny.

Dave: You can call from here.

Pam: No, you need some quiet time, and here comes the nurse with your breakfast. I'll be back in a few minutes.

Talk for a few minutes about how you felt while you were reading the conversation between Pam and Dave. Did you identify with what each of them was feeling? Saying? What would you have said differently? Would you have had a better plan for the day? Did you feel equally concerned for Dave and Pam in this moment of decision? Do you think the decision Dave urged them to make will cause any feelings of regret later? What else could they have done to be sure that "this is the right way to go" or to provide additional feelings of security for either of them?

As you think about health concerns and crises that might affect your own lives, it is important to prepare yourselves as much as possible to respond in the most appropriate and helpful ways. In most instances, you can do this by discussing the "what if" questions related to the potential health concern or crisis. For example, if an accident or serious illness is a concern, you might ask yourselves, "What if one of us was involved in a serious accident or was diagnosed with a life-threatening illness? What would we do first? Who would we call? Where would we find the best emergency care?" Remember that even if such a crisis never occurs, it is important to "be prepared."

One of the most obvious, yet most important ways to ensure immediate assistance in the event of a medical emergency is to post the telephone numbers of physicians, hospitals, the nearest relative or friend, and your pastor on a card next to the telephone. If and when such an emergency should occur, remember to stay as calm as possible and to "connect" with God immediately through prayer, even as you "connect" with others who can help.

Other significant questions you should explore together as objectively as possible include the following.

1. Do we or should we have a living will?
2. How much health insurance and life insurance do we currently have? Is it enough?
3. If we have children, who will care for them in the event of a tragedy that claims both our lives?
4. If one of us is diagnosed with a terminal illness, what arrangements should be made with HOSPICE or other caregivers?
5. In the event that one or both of us should die suddenly, do we have plans for organ donation, cremation, or traditional funeral and burial arrangements?

"In sickness and in health"—these words that are closely intertwined in the marriage covenant are experienced in the lives of all couples in varying degrees. Remember that a positive outlook, combined with a creative attitude, is the secret to a healthy approach to life. Specific plans for improving your health and specific steps toward the willingness to do so, accompanied by a continuing trust in God and daily prayers for God's blessing, are the keys that open the door to good results.

Devotional Thought: "Oh, restore me to health and make me live!" (Isaiah 38:16c).

Prayer: There are so many times, O God, when we need your healing in our lives. You know our concerns related to health and wholeness; help us to talk about them with each other. And help us take a close look at ourselves and seek your guidance and blessings, as we try to rid ourselves of all that is unhealthy and fills us with fear. Amen.

8. CHILDREN IN OUR CIRCLE OF LOVE

▼

If you have a child/children...

▲ consider exploring this chapter together in a setting that has special meaning for the two of you. Or, after reading through the chapter, make arrangements for the care of your child/children (as necessary) and go out for a special dinner or "fun date," choosing a place where you can complete the exercises and talk together.

▲ place a toy or other item belonging to your child/children beside your Bible as you begin, or if you are going out, take a picture of your child/children with you.

If you do not have a child/children...

▲ and do not plan to, skip to chapter 9.

▲ but would like to in the future, you might want to read part or all of this chapter in preparation, choosing which exercises you want to complete as you go along.

▲ and are undecided about whether you ever will, talk openly about this together now, sharing your thoughts, feelings, fears, hopes, and dreams. If there is any disagreement between you, turn to page 169 and complete the exercise "Ten Steps for Solving a Problem."

▲ because you are unable to physically, share your hopes and dreams and consider all your options. If you have not already done so, consult with doctors and counselors as appropriate. Remember that it can be extremely difficult to keep a marriage energized and growing when the process of having children becomes the focus of the marriage. If this is the case in your marriage, you might find it helpful to talk with a marriage counselor or your pastor.

1. Knit Your Family Together in Love

Devotional Thought: "This is my commandment, that you love one another as I have loved you" (John 15:12).
Prayer: Lord, show us how to love each other, even as you have loved us.

> Help us to be patient and kind with our children, just as you are patient and kind with us, your children. May this time we spend together bring new insights and understanding that will deepen our faith and expand our circle of love. Amen.

Have you ever had a sweater that was knitted so loosely that a snag, or even a big hole, was evident? Perhaps you've had another sweater that was closely knit, barely showing a snag. Similarly, a close-knit family has the strength and durability to withstand the "wear and tear" of life. A close-knit family, woven together with love, is our hope as parents. As we focus on weaving our families close together, however, we must remember that our children also need opportunities to grow and exercise their independence, so that eventually they are ready to leave the security of the family nest. Again, love is the thread that enables us to give our children space and, eventually, let go, allowing our children to become the persons God intends them to be.

There is no perfect marriage, and there are no perfect parents. We will make mistakes. But if we love each other and our children, imitating and sharing the love of Jesus Christ, they are more likely to grow up to be loving adults. The key is to love and respect each other and our children. Children learn primarily by example.

The best gift you can give your children is the example of your own strong, loving marriage. By showing your love for each other as well as for your children, you will help build their self-esteem and sense of security, and teach them how to be good spouses and parents in the future.

Many couples become so intent on meeting the daily responsibilities of caring for children and managing a family that they neglect their marriage relationship. Often this unhealthy practice begins when children are very young and demand more time and attention from their parents. Yet it is these early days of parenting when patterns are established that will affect not only the parent-child relationship but also the husband-wife relationship for many years to come.

Let's look in on a couple experiencing the joys of having a newborn, as well as the frustrations, particularly those related to time and energy levels. Janet and Steve have been married three years and are finding the adjustment to parenthood somewhat difficult, though they still are very much in love with each other.

It is the middle of the night. The house is dark, except for the tiny night light plugged into the outlet beside the crib in the corner of their bedroom. Steve and Jan are in a deep sleep. Steve has his arm around Jan, giving them a feeling of warmth and security they've experienced from the beginning of their marriage. Suddenly, a little cry pierces the silence.

Steve: Jan, wake up. The baby's awake.

Jan: W-what time is it?

Steve: (turning to look at the clock radio on the night stand) It's about 2:20.

Jan: I just fed her at 11:30. How can she be awake again? Can you feed her this time? I'm so tired.

Steve: I'm tired, too, Jan, and I've got a sales meeting at 8:00 this morning!

Jan: Okay, I'll feed her again, but I just haven't been able to get my strength back like I thought I would. I guess it takes longer after a C-section. I never knew having a baby would take so much energy. Since I'm not breast feeding, I thought we could share the night feedings.

Steve: I have been taking some of them, Jan. But just to show you that I'm concerned about you, I'll warm the bottle if you'll change her.

Jan: Thanks, sweetheart.

Steve: (returning with a warmed bottle) Here we are, Chloe, a nice warm snack in the middle of the night. (He looks at the bed and sees Jan with Chloe beside her. Chloe is awake, looking at him. Jan has fallen asleep.) Well, little angel, it looks like Daddy gets to feed you.

Jan awakens the next morning and glances at the clock. It's 6:15. Steve is just coming from the shower into the bedroom, wearing a towel. He reaches into the dresser drawer for shorts and socks.

Jan: Did you feed Chloe last night after all? I must have fallen asleep after I changed her.

Steve: I really didn't mind after I managed to wake up. We did some father-daughter bonding.

Jan: What am I going to do to get my energy level up, Steve?

Steve: (continues dressing) We'll manage somehow. I can help a little more, but I do have to go to Chicago tomorrow, you know, and I'll be gone overnight.

Jan: Maybe I should call my mother to come back and help for a few days, like she did at the beginning. She's only four hours away.

Steve: I think we should try to make it on our own. Your mother almost seems to take over at times. I know she means well, but I've seen how she makes you feel. It's like you lose your confidence in your ability to take care of Chloe.

Jan: You're right. I've got to learn to do it myself. I'll just let everything else go for a couple of days and take care of Chloe. (Steve—now wearing shorts, shirt, tie, and socks—walks to the closet to get his pants and shoes.) Steve, look down a minute.

Steve: Why? What's the matter?

Jan: You have two different socks on—one black and one brown! (Both laugh. Chloe wakes up.)

Steve: You know, we've got to laugh more!

Jan gets up, changes Chloe, and goes into the kitchen to get a bottle. When she returns, Steve is dressed for work.

Steve: I've got to go now.

Jan: But you haven't had any breakfast.

Steve: I'll pick up something at the deli on the way in. (Steve walks over to the bed, where Jan is feeding Chloe, and bends over to give Chloe a kiss on the forehead.) She's beautiful, isn't she?

Jan: She really is.

Steve: And so are you. I'll call you from the office.

It is now two days later. A ray of sunshine streams through the living room window like a ray of hope. Steve is returning from Chicago. He opens the front door and sees Jan and Chloe asleep in the rocking chair. Steve walks over to them and gently kisses Jan on the forehead.

Steve: Hi, honey.

Jan: Oh, Steve, you're home. I'm so glad. I didn't expect you so soon. I just fed Chloe. I was going to put something on for supper and straighten up a little before you got home.

Steve: I caught an earlier flight. And I stopped to get some Chinese food, so you won't have to cook. We'll have a party—just the three of us.

Jan: One of us needs to be changed first.

Steve: It looks like my timing was great. You warm up the Chinese and I'll change the one who needs changing.

After changing Chloe, Steve puts her in the battery-operated swing-bed, and she quickly goes back to sleep. Steve and Jan eat Chinese take-out on paper plates by candlelight.

Steve: This has been great. We've got to go out soon, though. We need some time by ourselves. How about getting a sitter next weekend?

Jan: Oh, I don't know, Steve. She's not even two months old yet.

Steve: Well, couldn't we go out for just a couple of hours and eat at our favorite restaurant? I was talking with Ken on the plane on the way back from Chicago, and he said that they found a wonderful baby-sitter for their two kids. She's a student at the community college and has all kinds of good references. How about it, Jan?

Jan: It seems so soon, but maybe. How about letting me think about it?

Talk together for a few minutes about the conversations of Jan and Steve. How are they attempting to adjust to parenthood and the new demands it is making on their time, their energy, and their relationship? What did they say or do to show their love for each other? For Chloe? What healthy patterns or habits are they establishing that will help to "knit their family together in love"? Is there anything that might be a real or potential threat to their relationship? What should they do about it? What else might they do to keep their marriage strong during this difficult life transition? How would you predict the future of their relationship as parents and as a couple? Do you see anything in their conversation that might help to enrich *your* marriage and *your* role as parents?

The importance of establishing a bond between parent and child is well documented. Perhaps the most dramatic examples of the bonding phenomenon can be seen in the animal world. Ducklings, for instance, follow their mother from birth. If the mother is not available, the ducklings will cling to another nurturing mother, such as a monkey, and follow that surrogate mother. Baby animals that are not loved become withdrawn and maladjusted. It is no different with human babies.

Parents (or other primary caregivers) must bond with their children by spending time with them and expressing love, in order for their children to learn to trust others—a very important first stage of development. True, it's never too late for parents to change their patterns of behavior and start hugging their children more. No matter what their age, children who are hugged usually end up returning hugs and "blossoming." It's much easier, however, to "bond" with children by forming healthy patterns of expressing love when they are young. This bonding experience continues for a lifetime as family members demonstrate love for one another through the years.

Just how do you keep love strong through the years—not only between yourselves as parents and your children, but also between yourselves as a couple? Let's look at each relationship separately, beginning with your relationship with your spouse "after kids."

Loving Your Spouse "After Kids"

When approached creatively, your relationship "after kids" can provide the basis for "the best that is yet to be." Only as you experience all of the "stages" of parenting, stretching over several decades, will you see the total picture of "married life with children." During these years, all kinds of challenges and threats to your relationship will occur at unexpected times. There also will be many special moments of joy and laughter and dreams coming true, creating an afterglow of love.

Continual *growth* is the key to developing a creative and satisfying relationship with each other "after kids"—as well as with your children. The physical growth of your children will bring both challenge and change, as will the growth of personal and family values and patterns of family responsibility—all directly influencing relationships within the family. The degree to which the two of you are able to grow in love and faith through these changes will determine the degree of love and faith within your children's lives.

Along your parenting journey, you also will discover that growth brings risks as dependence gives way to independence—beginning with the demanding days of infancy, through the turbulent teen years, until it's time to let go completely. Even then, you will find the need for continued growth—not only in understanding, accepting, and welcoming your adult children as they return home for brief or longer periods of time, but also in nurturing, caring, and loving each other when there's just the two of you again.

The important question, then, is *how* do you encourage continual growth in your marriage relationship "after kids"? The answer is by finding ways to give your relationship the time, attention, and energy it deserves. In light of the demands of parenting—not to mention the many other demands of life—this requires determination and creativity.

Having regular "time away"—both together and separately—will be important to your marriage relationship, whatever the ages of your children. This can happen only when both of you agree to take time for it! How can you do this while juggling daily demands and responsibilities? By scheduling these times as priorities in your busy schedules. You schedule times for doctor appointments and other important events on your calendars, so why not schedule time for a "date" together or some "space" alone? This really works. "Time away" becomes a priority rather than an option. Longer times away will require planning, including provisions for the extended care of children—perhaps with grandparents or trusted friends. Again, scheduling occasional getaways on your calendar will help make them priorities, as well as increase your anticipation of spending some special time together.

The opportunities for "time away" together are unlimited. Some inexpensive ideas include spending a half-day hiking or biking, seeing a movie at a bargain theater, taking a picnic lunch to a secluded park. Other possibilities that require a little more money and planning include an overnight stay at a resort, seeing a play, or saving up for dinner at a really fine restaurant.

If you are tempted to cancel a "date" or an extended time away, remind yourselves that these times help keep romance alive! What's more, the results are long-lasting, for your children as well as for yourselves. A strong, loving, romantic relationship between you and your spouse will "spill over" into the lives of your children, creating a healthy, happy home. Spending time together when your children are young also will help you to establish a hopeful, joyful relationship that will continue long after the kids have left home.

Loving Your Child

Children, like adults, need love. In extreme cases, whether or not children receive love may actually be a matter of life or death.

Mother Teresa carried many sick and dying babies and children from the filthy germ-infested streets of Calcutta into a simple home where they are cared for and loved. She knew that in order to survive, these malnourished children need love just as much as they need food. Today, compassionate, caring people come from all over the world to help feed, hold, love, and care for these little ones.

All children need love—not only to survive but also to *thrive*. Love gives a child lifelong self-esteem, confidence, and security. Love is the most important gift we can give our children. Unfortunately, many parents have difficulty expressing love. Perhaps they were not often shown affection as children and felt unloved—even though they might say, "I know my parents loved me." Or perhaps they felt loved as children only when they did what their parents wanted them to do. This is conditional love. The kind of love we are to give our children, however, is the kind of love God gives to us—*unconditional love.*

In other words, we are to love them at all times, regardless of what they may say or do. This does not mean that we must *approve* of everything they do. God does not approve of everything we do, yet God still loves us. In the same way, our children—whether they be toddlers or teens—need to know that we love them unconditionally.

How can you show unconditional love to your children? There are four primary ways.

1. Communicate with respect.

Your children need your respect—whether they are learning to walk or learning to drive. This is the way they learn to respect you and others. What does it mean to respect your children? In a nutshell, it is the golden rule: treating them as you would like to be treated. It means never calling your children "stupid" or telling them to "shut up" or saying things such as, "You never do anything right!" Such comments are destructive tapes that children begin playing in their minds again and again and continue playing throughout adulthood, hurting their self-esteem. Once "recorded" in a child's mind, these "tapes" are very difficult to eliminate. Remember, whatever you do not want your children to "replay" in their minds or say aloud to others are the very words you should not use when talking to your children.

2. Give encouragement.

Children of all ages need encouragement. Just think of how much you have benefited from the encouragement of your own parents and/or others through the years. Giving encouragement to young children is as simple as saying things such as, "I really like it when you help pick up your toys," or "I like the way you say 'please' and 'thank you'," or "I'm so glad God made you part of our family." As children grow older, let them express their dreams and hopes without discouraging them. Who knows, if they follow their dreams, they may find fulfillment! When they make mistakes, affirm them by saying things such as, "That sometimes happens. We all make mistakes at times," and "You do feel bad about that, don't you?" Let them talk about what happened without saying, "I told you so." Above all, let them know that you are interested in listening, and then *really listen*—without being critical or too quick to offer advice.

There are special times when children need encouragement, such as when your child comes home from school crying because some other child has hurt him or her physically or with words. Understanding and encouragement are very important then. Another time is when your family has moved, causing the tears and sadness of leaving friends in the community, school, and church. This too is a time when encouragement is especially needed.

3. Discipline with love.

The key word here is *love*. When a child feels loved, he or she learns to accept appropriate discipline as a necessary part of growing and learning. Although most children do not realize it and would never admit it, they actually need and *want* their parents to set boundaries and limits, which help to give them a sense of security. Because discipline is such a significant factor in the parent-child relationship, we will explore this in more detail later in the chapter, suggesting some basic ways you can "discipline with love."

4. *Spend time with your children.*

Many parents today try to compensate for the lack of time they spend with their children by buying them things or enrolling them in various lessons, classes, or other "opportunities." Yet, the truth is, *there is no substitute for the time a child spends with his or her parents.* Taking time to be with your children—despite busy schedules—says more about your love for them than words ever could.

Be intentional about having regular "family time"—time when the whole family can enjoy being together. It doesn't matter what you choose to do; the important thing is simply that you spend time together. Turn to page 136 for some suggestions of family traditions; you might find some new ideas you'd like to add to your family's list of favorite things to do together.

It also is important to spend time with each child, giving some "one on one" time while your spouse or another relative or friend is with the other children. Many parents find that when they regularly give this kind of undivided attention to a child—even if only for brief periods of time, such as in the morning or evening—he or she generally has a better disposition and is more content to play alone or with siblings or other children. Teens also need time with each parent, which allows them to feel important and "open up" as they explore special interests or concerns with one parent or the other. Here are just a few ideas for spending "one on one" time with a child—from infants to teens. (Note: Some of these ideas also may be fun for the entire family.)

▲ Talk to your baby as you hold him or her; make your baby feel secure from the very beginning!
▲ Dance together as soon as your child can walk. Sing "Here We Go Round the Mulberry Bush" and gently fall down together.
▲ Cuddle your child as you read books or stories.
▲ Have your child assist you in the kitchen—stirring, measuring, decorating cakes, setting the table—and appreciate his or her efforts.
▲ Make heart-shaped sandwiches; decorate hamburgers with funny faces using ketchup, mustard, pickles, onions, or other garnishes.
▲ Sing silly songs, such as "I Love You a Bushel and a Peck" or "Skinna marinka dinky doo, skinna marinka do, I love you." Or make up your own songs, such as "I love you Jessica. Yes, I do. Love, kisses, and hugs all for you." Any tune will do!
▲ Work together to make a scrapbook/album of your child's drawings, art projects, photos, keepsakes, and so forth.
▲ Fill a jar with little notes (or pictures) suggesting things you might do together, such as "Go for a walk," "Read a book," "Blow bubbles," or "Ride a bike." Pick an idea from the jar and do it! (Note: You might like to add other suggestions, such as "Kiss your mommy or daddy" and "Let's hug.")

▲ Spell "I love you" and other messages with alphabet cereal or soup.

▲ Enjoy a special or "favorite" meal together—at home or at a restaurant. You might try a different food—Mexican, Chinese, Italian, and so forth—each time.

▲ Have a picnic—outside or inside! Let your child help gather or prepare food and other items. All ages enjoy picnics!

▲ Kisses and hugs are needed at every age, even though teenagers may shy away from them for a while.

▲ Find a hobby or sport or "shared interest" you can enjoy together.

▲ Take your son or daughter to work with you, or ask him or her to help you with a special project you are working on.

▲ Sit on the bed together at the end—or beginning—of the day and talk for a while.

▲ Just take time to listen, listen, listen!

It's important to remember that children and teens also need some time alone—without a parent or others constantly entertaining them. Of course, playing with other children—or spending time with other teens—encourages social skills and enhances self-esteem; and children of all ages need interaction with peers and others outside the family in order to develop healthy relationships. Still, children need time alone just as adults do. Young children need nap times or quiet times as well as time for playing by themselves. Learning to look at books, color, or play quietly for short periods of time while parents are busy helps children develop self-esteem as they gain a sense of independence and initiative. Likewise, teens need privacy and time alone to think and dream as they grow more and more independent.

Time with family, time with each parent, time with friends, and time alone: All contribute to a happy, healthy child—and a happy, healthy family.

Take a few moments now to measure your "love factor" with your children. In order to be as objective as you can, be sure to do this when you are away from your children or when they are asleep. Begin by talking about these questions:

▲ How do you remember your parents expressing love to you?
▲ Were these good examples of love?
▲ Did both your mother and father show you enough love?
▲ What were the ways you were disciplined as a child?
▲ Which was most effective?
▲ Do you feel your parents were fair or too strict?
▲ Do the two of you agree about how you should "train [your] children in the right way, and when old, they will not stray" (Proverbs 22:6)?

Complete the following "love factor" inventory to see how you're doing now and to discover what things you're currently not doing that you would like to do in the future. Some answers may depend on the age(s) of your child/children.

Measuring Our Love Factor with Our Children

YES	NO	
___	___	Do we hug/touch/kiss our child/children? (How frequently?)
___	___	Do we each spend time alone with each child, helping us to realize that he/she is a unique creation?
___	___	Do we go *with* our child/children to church and/or Sunday school?
___	___	Do we show respect for each other in front of our child/children?
___	___	Do we give loving attention to our child/children at bedtime?
___	___	Do we read the Bible to or with our child/children?
___	___	Is our "training" or discipline appropriate to the age(s) and acts of our child/children?
___	___	Are we careful not to compare one child to another?
___	___	Do we really listen to the little things, as well as the more important things, that our child/children tell(s) us?
___	___	Do we tell our child/children that we love him/her/them, even when we don't like what he/she/they have done?
___	___	Do we take time to play or have fun with our child/children?
___	___	Do we let our child/children gain independence as appropriate?
___	___	Have we had a family party recently?
___	___	Do we hug each other in front of our child/children?
___	___	Do we laugh together as a family?
___	___	Do we as a family help other people, such as neighbors and people in need?
___	___	Do we admit to our child/children when we are wrong?
___	___	Do we ask our child/children for forgiveness?
___	___	Do we pray for and with our child/children?

A Special Word for Blended Families

Blended families are very common today. Most often, divorce is a factor, and children generally spend alternate weekends with each parent. Sometimes parents have joint custody of their children—with both parents taking care of the children separately yet, supposedly, equally. Both situations have the potential of being very trying and difficult for everyone involved.

Handling the dynamics of a blended family requires a great deal of patience and understanding, as well as a nonjudgmental, cooperative approach. When there has been a divorce, it is beneficial to everyone involved if the parents are able to talk about their children and make plans in a friendly, respectful manner. It also is important not to talk about the other parent as the "bad guy"—even if true—as this is often very disturbing and confusing to children. Likewise, it is helpful not to criticize the stepmother or stepfather in front of the children, for it is in the best interest of the children to accept and be accepted by both sets of caregivers.

Even adult children are affected when their parents divorce and remarry. Just as divorce is very difficult for children who are still living at home, it also can be very difficult for adult children—even though they are mature enough to understand the circumstances. Though they may not live under the same roof with a stepparent or stepbrothers and stepsisters, adult children must adjust to new family dynamics. In either case, understanding is the key to helping family members grow together in love.

Regardless of the family makeup, a close-knit family is knit together in love. If love is the thread that holds our families together, then what are the "weaving tools" we should use as we strive to create beautiful, enduring families? In other words, how do we channel and express our love in ways that will help to make our families strong? We have already explored a few of these; now let us take a closer look at three very important ways you can strengthen your family in love.

2. Three Ways to a Stronger Family

Disciplining in Love

Let's look in on Jan and Steve again. It is seven years later. In a few weeks, they will celebrate their tenth anniversary. Chloe is now seven, and she has a brother, Jamie, age five, and a sister, Heidi, age three. Although the children get along fairly well, they are typical children, needing guidance and direction. As a result, Jan and Steve find themselves experiencing some tension on a daily basis. Some of it is simply the result of "too much to do and not enough time." Some of it, however, is due to unresolved questions and issues related to the way they discipline the children. Their ideas about discipline are quite different, in fact, and the cause of frequent arguments, which often are overheard by the children.

Jan is working full time; Steve is traveling more. Chloe is in second grade, excelling as a student; Jamie, who is beginning kindergarten, seems to have a learning disability; Heidi is going through a period of separation anxiety, crying when she is left at day care. In the afternoons after school, Ginny, a sitter, comes to stay with Chloe and Jamie until Jan comes home with Heidi.

It is a typical Friday evening. Jan has returned home at 5:00 P.M., Ginny has gone, and Chloe and Jamie are fighting over which TV program to watch. Five minutes later, Steve arrives home.

Steve: Hi, everybody. I'm home. *(Chloe and Jamie are fighting over the remote control, shouting, "It's my turn!")* Hey, wait a minute. How come you're watching TV on such a nice day? You should be outside playing!" *(Steve turns to Jan, who is beginning to prepare supper in the kitchen.)* Jan, I thought we agreed we wouldn't let them watch TV after school—with only one show after supper.

Jan: Steve, I can't control *everything*. I had a rough day at work. Ginny let them watch for the last hour, and today I just can't handle the hassle of getting three children outside when they are quiet watching television.

Steve: Well, they're not quiet now!

Jan: Then *you* take over! You're the one who lets them do what they want most of the time. You seem to be so upset about them watching TV, but you let them get away with lots of other things!

Steve: Okay, okay. We don't always agree about disciplining the kids, but it isn't good for them to spend so much time just sitting in front of the television. Come on, you three. We're going to play Frisbee for twenty minutes, and then we're coming in to help Mom finish getting ready for supper. You get the Frisbee, Jamie. Chloe, you get jackets for yourself and Heidi. I'll meet you in the backyard! (Steve flips off the TV, motions the children out, and kisses Jan lightly on the forehead as he walks out.) I'm sorry, honey.

It's now 9:30 P.M. The children are in bed. Jan and Steve usually watch a sitcom at this time but they know that tonight they need to talk instead.

Steve: We've got to get together on running this household, Jan. I didn't mean to react so loudly about the TV, but I think we have to limit the time the kids spend just sitting in front of it, watching some stupid show.

Jan: I agree, Steve, but sometimes it's easier just to let them watch it, especially after Ginny has told them they could.

Steve: Well, that's a problem we can solve by informing Ginny that she just can't do that. We're paying her to care for the kids and follow our directions!

Jan: We don't want to lose her, though!

Steve: Of course not. Let me handle it. But that isn't our main problem. We have to agree about more things. We just don't seem to be on the same wavelength when it comes to raising the kids. You say I'm too lenient a lot of the time, and I say they need to develop as normal

Jan: kids—without sitting around watching life on a 21-inch screen!

Jan: Well, you're just not very consistent, Steve. I want to discipline them by having them clean up their rooms and take their shoes off when they come inside and remember their manners when my parents come, and you just let those things go. You're always saying, "They're growing up," Jan. Don't be too hard on them. Ignore the little things and focus on life. I believe they need rules, discipline. That's the way I grew up.

Steve: But if we're too strict, we won't have the relaxed spirit we've always said we wanted to have in our family. What's the difference if the house isn't so neat or the floor gets tracked up once in a while?

Jan: I just wish we could be consistent, Steve. That's all. And I wish we had a plan for the week—who's doing what and when. So much of the time our life is too chaotic, trying to get the children to all the places they have to go and barely making connections—not to mention feeling exhausted and never having any time for ourselves.

Steve: That's something I'd like to work on, too. It seemed so much easier when Chloe was a baby, but even then it was hard to find time for us. Remember those days?

Jan: Yes, and I always thought it would be easier once the children were in school! Just think of all the extra things they're involved in besides school. Chloe's taking violin lessons, Jamie's swimming three times a week—and it looks like he's going to need some tutoring when he gets into first grade—and all three of them are involved in choir practice and Sunday school programs.

Steve: And now Chloe wants to join a Brownie troop, and Heidi has been asked to be part of that dance group. Where does it stop?

Jan: It doesn't stop. Steve, *We* have to stop and take a look at how we can really enjoy these kids. You always used to say, "The honeymoon isn't over." Well, maybe it is.

Steve: Never! We'll just have to reorganize our lives a bit. Maybe we can go to that parenting class the church is offering. I think it starts next month. We could go to those six sessions and then take off for our tenth anniversary when your parents come for that long weekend. The honeymoon must go on!

Jan: You're incorrigible, Steve.

Steve: I know.

Much of Jan and Steve's conversations had to do with discipline. But just what is discipline? Many parents have a narrow definition of discipline, limiting it to punishment or consequences for misbehavior. The truth is that discipline sets limits for children and helps them to function not only within their families but also within society, as they realize that the world does not revolve around them. Children and teens who are disciplined in love do not try to "rule" their parents and families or disrupt their classrooms in school.

A recent article in *The Washington Post* notes that with so much emphasis being placed today on promoting students' self-esteem, teachers and educators often are afraid to discipline or demand good behavior because they are afraid they will be accused of damaging students' self-esteem (May 19, 1997, C5). Unfortunately, many parents fall into the trap of this kind of thinking as well. The result, some suggest, is a generation of ill-behaved kids. Actually, loving discipline helps, not hinders, self-esteem by teaching children to respect others and to realize that no one is above the consequences of his or her actions. Loving discipline, then, enables children to become productive participants in their families, schools, communities, and in later years, work environments.

What does it mean to discipline in love? First, it means treating children with respect—living by the golden rule. Second, it means being fair—ensuring that boundaries and consequences for misbehavior are appropriate to children's ages and understanding. Finally, it is assuring children that they are loved at all times and in all circumstances—not because of what they do, but because of who they are.

Of these three guidelines, parents often have most difficulty in establishing fair and appropriate boundaries and consequences. Actually, setting appropriate boundaries does not give parents as much trouble as determining appropriate consequences. Obviously, not every method is appropriate for every age. Parents must be flexible and make adjustments as their children grow in age and responsibility.

Our intent is not to provide an exhaustive discussion of parental discipline; there are numerous excellent books devoted to that subject, some of which we mention in the bibliography. It may be helpful, however, to include here some basics related to age-appropriate strategies, particularly as related to consequences for ignoring or disobeying established boundaries.

Let us begin by acknowledging that an infant does not need discipline. As every parent knows all too well, all babies cry; it is their primary means of communication. Babies cry when they are hungry, wet, tired, hot, cold, hurting, lonely, frustrated—the list goes on and on. Their cries, then, signal specific needs. Meeting the basic needs of their children and providing lots of love are two of the most important tasks parents have in the early months of their children's lives. Once a secure "foundation" of love and trust has been built in these early months, parents can slowly begin to respond less quickly to their children's cries when they know that all their basic needs have been met. For example, if a parent knows that a child is not in pain and has been fed and changed, he or she may let the child cry in the crib for a few minutes before returning to reassure the child of his or her presence by patting, singing, or talking to the child.

With young children, "time out" often is an effective disciplinary response. Experts generally agree it is most effective to send a child to the same location for each "time out," keeping all toys or other desirable objects away from the child. Equally important are making sure that the child understands why he or she is being given a "time out" and reassuring the child that he or she is loved. When a child is unable to control his or her behavior, he or she may need to spend time alone in another room, away from all other family members and all activity, until he or she calms down. This is especially helpful with tantrums, which usually are intended for the benefit of an audience.

Whatever the age, spanking usually is not a helpful means of discipline, although there is some difference of opinion about this. Generally speaking, other disciplinary measures are more appropriate and effective than spanking. Of course, there are a few rare exceptions, such as when spanking a child on the seat may help the child to recognize and avoid physical danger. Frequent spanking, however, loses its effectiveness and can damage a child's self-esteem. Hitting or slapping a child in anger is never acceptable. Abuse can result when children are spanked too hard and too frequently or hurt physically in the name of discipline. Also, they frequently grow up to become abusive parents.

With older children and teens, taking away privileges is an extremely effective consequence for misbehavior. It is important, however, that the privilege be taken away for an appropriate length of time. "Grounding" a child or teen for several weeks for committing a minor infraction, for example, is hardly fair and can cause more disobedience on the part of the child or teen. On the other hand, refraining from disciplining a child or teen because he or she is threatening rebellious behavior or is going through a "difficult time" can lead to even more problems.

The "Difficult Times"

As odd as it may sound, discipline can actually help you and your family make it through the difficult times. When are the difficult times?

▲ Your two-year-old throws frequent temper tantrums as he or she explores boundaries and struggles to gain more independence.
▲ You do not have enough money for the clothes your son or daughter feels are necessary to be accepted and "keep up" with peers.
▲ Your child is hanging around with the "wrong crowd" and getting into trouble.
▲ Your teenagers are struggling to find their identity and are caught up in what their peers are doing or not doing.

These are just some of the many trying times you may experience as a family. In times like these, "loving understanding" discipline can help you and your children grow closer together by assuring them of your love. Again, if children are allowed "free reign," they do not feel protected from their own impulses.

As we've said, loving discipline helps children—whatever their age—to know their boundaries and to say "no" to peers, giving them the courage to do the right thing. It also encourages children to be less self-absorbed and more generous with others. All these are important "values" that help children to weather difficult times.

Sometimes the most difficult times a family encounters are not the result of the children but the result of a poor marriage relationship. Unfortunately, some couples who are having problems believe that their children will be "better off" if they divorce. In most cases, however, the children—whether they are toddlers or teens—have problems after their parents divorce. Some children feel responsible for their parents' divorce; others feel a great sense of sadness and loss when family members are pulled apart. In either case, it is not unusual for the unhappiness and inner turmoil of the children to surface as discipline problems.

One seven-year-old boy wrote these words after his parents divorced:

> One day my dad [and mom] had a divorce
>   and he broke the force.
> He had a friend and tried to start over
>   and went to the end.
> I'm okay. I won't have a cow.
> I wonder what he's thinken about now.
> All I know is he messed up his life
>   and now he aint got no wife.

But that little boy wasn't "okay." He had trouble sleeping, had nightmares, and didn't do well in school. It took several years for him to get over his sadness, hurt, anger, and feelings of being lost.

Though there are some situations and relationships that cannot be mended—such as situations involving continual physical or mental abuse—most couples can work out their problems and differences if they are committed to each other in love and are willing to work at their relationship—especially through the difficult times. Although some couples feel a divorce is in the best interest of the children, children generally suffer—even in the best of situations—when their parents divorce. Working to mend the relationship is usually best. As we've said, the greatest investment a couple can make for the children in their circle of love is to love each other and keep from breaking the threads that hold them together "as long as [they] both shall live." Discipline and commitment, centered in love—God's love—are the keys that make this possible.

In her book *What Is a Family?* Edith Schaeffer describes the family as a mobile. A mobile can be made from various materials—copper, brass, wrought iron, metal, wood, or glass—all of which are held together by almost invisible threads. Regardless of the materials that hold it together, this work of art is blown by the wind—constantly twisting, turning, moving, changing. In like manner, the gentle breeze of the Holy Spirit can blow through a family, producing great beauty.

When the strong winds blow, threatening to break our families apart just as the pieces of a mobile can be shattered in a storm, we must call upon the gentle breeze of the Spirit to blow through our family, enabling us to weather even the most difficult times.

Growing Together in Faith

Another important way to strengthen your family is to grow together in faith. In fact, this alone can do more to strengthen your family than anything else. The most important growth that takes place in any family is spiritual growth—the kind of growth that comes from believing and talking about God together, praying together, celebrating God's guidance together, reading the Bible together, and going to church together. These things will help you and your children know that God cares for your family—and each individual within it—as a loving parent cares for a child, giving your family a sense of security and love and hope.

Growing in faith as a family requires a discipline that all too often is overlooked in the busyness of family life; it means you must take some time every day to focus on God *together.* Yet focusing on God as a family doesn't have to be complicated or time-consuming. Even the simple act of saying or singing a prayer before meals is one of the most meaningful ways to involve your children—whatever their ages—in talking to God.

Bedtime prayers are another good way to teach children to talk to God. Young children may recite a simple prayer, such as "Now I Lay Me Down to Sleep," or—like older brothers and sisters—share their own thoughts about the day, expressions of trust, and requests for help and thanksgiving for family and friends. Whatever their age, always encourage your children to pray as if they are talking to God in an everyday conversation, and never laugh at their expressions—as humorous as they may be—or insist that they read or memorize long prayers. Sharing faith as a family in these and other ways will bring spiritual growth as you grow closer to God and closer together.

Another important and creative way to encourage spiritual growth within your family is to share faith with others in the larger family we call "church." Sunday school classes, children's choirs, youth programs, outreach opportunities, Sunday worship—all help to strengthen belief and give confidence to children and youth as part of God's family. When your children worship with others their own age—along with you and all the other parents—they experience an awareness of something significant happening. It is as if a voice inside them says, "This is good. God is good. I feel good to be part of this." Unless you set the example, however, through your own participation in worship and other programs and service opportunities of the church, your children's participation will not be as effective. The old saying is true: Seeing is believing.

Participating in the church is an important "faith ritual" for your family, reminding you of God's love and protection. Other family "faith rituals" also can serve as reminders of God's constant care for your family. Seasonal preparations for Christmas and Easter, for example, can be very meaningful. Some families read the stories of Jesus' birth and resurrection at these times; others act out the stories in a family circle, each person taking the role of a biblical character.

Another "faith ritual" in some families is the "blessing cup," reserved for special occasions in the family circle—birth, baptism, confirmation, graduation, or marriage, as well as celebrations for receiving an award or scholarship or beginning a new job. Each family member drinks from the "blessing cup," symbolizing his or her participation in the blessing of God—"My cup overflows" (Psalm 23:5).

Your family can grow in faith and sustain that faith through these and other special family "faith rituals"—some passed on from one generation to the next; others created by you and your family. Like "faith rituals," family traditions can strengthen your family as you set aside time simply to celebrate and share the gift of family.

Creating Family Traditions

Devotional Thought: "Let the little children come to me" (Matthew 19:14).

If Jesus, who was so busy doing God's work, encouraged the children to come to him, so too we, who have jobs and other commitments, must be careful to allow time for our children to come to us. We must listen to them and let them know by our words and actions that we love them.

Prayer: Lord, thank you for our children. Help us never to be too busy to listen and to give the unconditional love and acceptance they need. May we be more like you, who accepted and loved all people, even when they did something wrong. Amen.

As we mentioned earlier in this chapter, spending time with your children—individually and as a family—is extremely important to the well-being of your children as well as the "health" of your family. Certainly this time does not need to be planned or structured; some of the most memorable times you will ever spend with your children may be spontaneous. As we've seen, however, there is great meaning and power in ritual. Children love repetition; adults also are creatures of habit.

The things your family chooses to do again and again not only will build and strengthen relationships but also will shape and define who you are as a family and what is important to you. Family traditions, then, are the building blocks of your unique "family identity." Your children will carry these traditions and the family identity created by them throughout their lives, someday perhaps choosing to pass many of them on to their own families.

What traditions did your family have when you were growing up—for birthdays, holidays, and other times? Talk together about some of these now.

Which of these traditions are you continuing or would you like to continue? Are there others that you would like to start with your children? What traditions have you heard about that sound fun and helpful to building a strong family? What about some of these?

▲ Make a "birthday book" for each child. Each year on the child's birthday, write a letter to the child to be placed in the book, including "highlights" or important and interesting events of the year, as well as photos or artwork of the child.

▲ When the child is old enough, let him or her choose the menu or restaurant for a special birthday dinner.

▲ Give your child/children homemade coupons for special events or "treats," such as "a trip to the zoo" or "lunch out with Dad or Mom."

▲ Have a regular time for sharing "the best time of the week"—such as on Friday or Saturday evening. Or, each night before tucking your child/children into bed, share "the best time of the day." This will help you to put everything into perspective and find something good even in a difficult day or week.

▲ At Christmas time, make being together as a family more important than receiving gifts. Do things for others, such as giving toys or food to families in need. Each night during the Christmas season, or on Christmas Eve only, light a candle or candles before bedtime and share a carol and prayer in the candlelight.

▲ On Christmas Day, consider re-telling the Christmas story before opening gifts. Then, distribute gifts one-by-one, to create special meaning for each member of the family.

▲ Collect stories about memorable times, such as being snowed in by a blizzard, getting lost on a trip, or having to do everything by candlelight when the power went out one night. Retell these stories through the years.

▲ Make animal pancakes or cookies with the children on Saturdays and/or special occasions.

▲ Work together to put photos into albums on special holidays.

▲ Encourage your child/children to make up plays and present them for the family.

▲ Read a book together at night or at other times. When children are older, read portions of a longer book until you complete it.

▲ Think about special or unique traditions from your childhood that you might like to continue—such as eating "fastnachts" (doughnuts) at Lent (a Pennsylvania tradition).

▲ Ask your child/children to suggest new traditions *they* would like to begin!

Remember, as you show your love for each other as husband and wife and your love for your children, you become role models of loving mates and parents, teaching your children how to love and building their sense of self-worth. Love is the greatest gift (1 Corinthians 13:13)!

© 1996 Bil Keane, Inc. Dist. by Cowles Synd., Inc.

9. MIRACLE GROW

▼

As you begin this chapter
▲ place a plant—perhaps one that is blooming—before you as a visual reminder that your marriage must be cared for and nurtured in order to grow.
▲ consider planting a few seeds or plants together (depending on the time of year and the climate of your area) and watch them grow in the weeks ahead, symbolizing continual growth in your marriage.
▲ enjoy a cup of herbal tea or a fruit drink together—just for fun!

1. How Does Our Marriage Grow?

Devotional Thought: "Your faith is growing abundantly, and . . . love . . . is increasing" (2 Thessalonians 1:3*b*). Just as a healthy plant continues to grow, so you can continue to grow in marriage. As you grow closer to God, you will grow closer to each other. As your faith increases, your love will increase—not suddenly, but gradually.

Prayer: Lord, help us to nurture our love so that it may grow. Amen.

With the proper nutrients, adequate water and sunlight, fertile soil, and attentive care, a budding plant will continue to grow, eventually blossoming in full beauty. Without nurturing care, however, the plant will wither and die.

So it is in marriage. But just how do you "nurture" your marriage? Take turns completing the following sentences:

I feel nurtured (loved) when you . . .

I think I could nurture our marriage and help it grow by . . .

I think my spouse could nurture our marriage and help it grow by . . .

Now take turns completing the following "miracle grow" inventory, writing the appropriate number in each blank and covering the responses of your partner as necessary.

Miracle Grow Inventory

frequently - 5   occasionally - 3   never - 1

His Response   Her Response

_____	_____	How often do you "play" together and have fun?
_____	_____	How often do you spend time together when you are not at work?
_____	_____	Do you help your partner when he/she is anxious or worried?
_____	_____	Do you listen and welcome different opinions without becoming upset?
_____	_____	How often do you hug and hold hands (unrelated to love-making)?
_____	_____	Do you respect your partner's need for time alone?
_____	_____	Do you try to accept your partner's friends and family, even if it's difficult?
_____	_____	How often do you show your partner that you care?
_____	_____	Do you spend adequate time with your partner, in relation to the amount you spend with your friends and other family members?
_____	_____	How often do you nurture yourselves spiritually?

How do you evaluate your Miracle Grow Inventory and the growth of your marriage? Your "scoring key" might look something like this: If each of you had a total of 35-50, you are doing well. If one or both of you scored 30 or less, you may need a little "miracle grow." If you did not agree with some of your partner's responses, it would be helpful to talk about this. Also, take a look at how many questions each of you answered with a "1" and identify how you might grow in these areas.

This exercise is not meant to make you critical or to start an argument, but to help you see creative possibilities for growth in your relationship. Throughout this book, you have been exploring various ways to nurture your marriage. All are important, but perhaps none is more important to the growth of your marriage than *spiritual* nourishment.

2. Growing Our Marriage with Spiritual Nourishment

> **Devotional Thought:** "They are like trees planted by streams of water" (Psalm 1:3).
>
> Can you see a tree from where you are now—whether you are sitting outside or looking through the nearest window? Is it growing near water? To be healthy, it needs water—either from rain or nearby streams or rivers. If there are no trees nearby, think for a moment about the beauty of trees and the importance of their roots for bringing nourishment. In the same way, your lives—as individuals and as a couple—need to be nourished spiritually.
>
> **Prayer:** Dear God, help us to think about how we can nourish the "roots" of our marriage as we relate to each other and to you. Amen.

The directions on the Miracle Grow plant fertilizer read: "Apply liberally around the roots of plants." Similarly, you fertilize your marriage when you give prayerful attention to the "roots" of your marriage—the deep beliefs, values, and commitments that connect you to God and God's creative power to strengthen your life together. One of the best ways to "grow" your marriage is to nurture it spiritually.

Meet Steve, Debbie, Sara, and Jody—a seemingly "happy family" who are caring for one another and enjoying their life together day-by-day. Steve and Debbie have been married for eight years. Jody, age six, and Sara, age four, feel secure in their home, having lived in the same house since birth. All of them are involved in church on a regular basis, attending worship services and Sunday school. Yet despite all appearances, something seems to be missing.

It is Sunday afternoon and they are driving home from church. Tune in to their conversation as they share some of their feelings.

Steve: I didn't get the point of Pastor Young's sermon today. Why was he comparing Jesus' growing-up years to our lives? It just seemed irrelevant to me. We live in such a different world.

Debbie: Your mind must have been wandering when he talked about inner growth. He said we need to grow in our faith—just as children need to grow in so many ways—in order to be able to live life to the fullest.

Sara: I'm growing bigger.

Debbie: Of course you are, honey.

Jody: My Sunday school teacher said we should grow up to be like Jesus.

Steve: That's true, Jody. Adults try to grow to be like Jesus too but sometimes it's not easy—especially when you feel like you're already "grown up."

Jody: Are you going to grow any bigger, Daddy?

Steve: There's not much chance that I'll grow any taller, Jody, but I can grow in the ways Mom was talking about.

Jody: I bet I'll be taller than you, Dad.

Steve: We'll see, but the most important thing is not how tall you are; it's being your best at whatever age or height you are.

Sara: Daddy, can we stop at McDonalds?

Steve: No, we're not stopping at McDonalds today.

Sara: But I want a Happy Meal!

Debbie: We're going to have a "happy meal" at home! You and Jody are going to help me get it ready while Daddy takes the flowers from church to the nursing home.

Steve: (pulling into their driveway) Okay, guys. Here we are. You two help Mom with dinner. I'll be back in about twenty minutes. We'll have time to go to the park later on this afternoon.

Two hours later, Sara is taking a nap and Jody is playing with his friend Scotty. Debbie is paying bills, and Steve is balancing the checkbook. Steve looks up for a moment, as if trying to decide whether to say what's on his mind. Read the following dialogue as if you are Debbie and Steve.

Steve: Can we talk, Debbie?

Debbie: Sure. What's up? Checkbook problem?

Steve: No, I'm just thinking about our conversation in the car on the way home from church.

Debbie: What?

Steve: Well, I'm wondering if I've stopped growing—you know, spiritually. Maybe both of us should be growing more—in our faith.

Debbie: I kind of feel that same way. We seem to be exactly where we were four or five years ago—like we've reached a plateau or something. We go to church most Sundays, but I must admit I don't put myself into what's happening in worship. I'm just happy to sit and relax a while.

Steve: You know, I've always thought that Sunday school was for kids, and that once you're grown, you've "arrived." But maybe we haven't.

Debbie: What can we do? How can we grow?

Steve: The question is, *When?* We're so busy with work and the kids, trying to be good parents. It seems like there's no time left.

Debbie: Well, maybe we could get involved in that new study group at the church. It starts next month. I think it's called "How Is Your Devotional Life These Days?"

Steve: I don't like those groups. Everybody tries to impress everyone else with what they know and how they've "grown in the faith." I don't know as much about the Bible and faith as a lot of them, and I don't want to be embarrassed.

Debbie: But you don't need to be embarrassed, Steve. The most important thing is being willing to say who you are and where you are in your faith. Nobody has all the answers. The fact that we want to grow is the key—along with knowing that we need God's help. I know I need to grow a lot more spiritually.

Steve: I guess you're right. I really want to grow, and I want the kids to see what's happening in our lives too. I want them to know that they can grow spiritually as well as physically. I want them to have the kind of faith that makes them feel loved and self-assured.

Debbie: Me too, and I think the important thing is knowing there are possibilities. We can change and grow. That's a miracle in itself!

Steve: When do we start? I want to be excited about my faith again, and I don't want us to wait until we're retired to start enjoying life—really living. Wasn't it Browning who wrote, "Come along, grow old with me/ The best of life is yet to be"? The best of life doesn't have to be way off in the future.

Debbie: But maybe that's part of it, Steve. At least with God guiding us, there's always the hope of a better life—don't you think?

Pause now for a few minutes to reflect on your own life. Does something seem to be missing from your life? In what ways have you grown spiritually—as individuals and as a couple—in the past few years? How has your understanding of faith changed in relation to everyday life, as well as to crises you've experienced along the way? Do you see new "leaves" sprouting in your marriage? Do you need to apply some "Miracle Grow"? If so, how?

The following Spiritual Growth Tree diagram is provided to help you reflect further on these questions. Steve and Debbie found this to be very helpful, defining their past, present, and future spiritual growth. You may work together, diagramming your spiritual growth as a couple, or you may make a copy of the diagram and complete the exercise individually. If you choose to work together, you might use different colored pens or pencils to identify your individual growth patterns.

On the *solid-line roots* of the tree, write the experiences in your early lives—and perhaps in the early days or years of your marriage—that caused your "spiritual roots" to form and grow, later producing "leaves" or "fruit" in your lives. Debbie and Steve's diagram included things such as going to youth camp and Sunday school, saying bedtime prayers, listening to Bible stories told by Grandmother, and taking a college Bible course. On the *solid-line branches* of the tree, name the various "fruits" or outcomes of these spiritual roots—in relation to God and to others. Debbie and Steve's branches named "fruits" such as having a basic faith in God, attending Sunday school and church regularly, learning to control anger, and loving and caring for others.

Now, on the *dotted-line roots* of the tree, write those "hoped for" spiritual roots—in other words, the things you plan to do individually or together in order to deepen your faith and grow spiritually. Debbie and Steve listed the following: joining a group Bible study, having a regular quiet time with God, beginning family devotions, singing in the choir, and teaching high school boys/teaching children Bible songs and stories. Likewise, on the *dotted-line branches*, write the "fruits" or outcomes you expect to be evident in your life after you "extend your spiritual roots." For Debbie and Steve, expected "fruits" including listening to God, knowing and doing God's will, sharing faith with others, being more joyful, and growing closer as a family.

It is our hope that this exercise has helped you to identify some of the ways you can grow spiritually. Let's take a closer look at some specific things you can do to "feed" your marriage as well as your souls.

3. Guidelines for Feeding Our Marriage and Our Souls

Cultivating a Devotional Life: Feeding Roots and Foliage

Cultivating a devotional life is one of the most effective ways to nurture spiritual growth. Unfortunately, in our fast-paced society, this is one of the most neglected disciplines of the spiritual life. Yet only by taking the time to nurture the roots of your marriage, which connect you to God and thus to each other, can you grow strong enough to weather the difficult circumstances that may come along during your life together.

What are you doing now to cultivate a devotional life? Some couples have a shared "quiet time" when they read from the Bible and/or devotional materials and pray together. Others choose to do this separately. Still others have a separate quiet time but read the same material, coming together afterward to share their thoughts and pray together. Many devotional materials are available, for individuals as well as for couples. (See the bibliography for suggested devotional books *for couples*.) Take time to review some of these and others you may find at a local bookstore, and choose the one that's right for you. As you reconsider your needs, interests, and progress from time to time, you may want to look for another resource that will help to deepen your spiritual journey.

You also might want to purchase a simple notebook or blank "journal" to use for recording reflections on Scripture passages and devotional readings, prayers, specific prayer requests, answers to prayer; and other observations related to your spiritual journey. If, for example, your devotional reading for the day is about change, you might record your thoughts about change as it relates to your life at the present moment. Your journal entry might read something like this:

Lord, today as I face my work, I realize I have difficulty with a coworker who seems to be critical of me. Help me try to understand that something may be bothering this person; or, if there really are changes I need to make in myself or the work I do, help me see these needs. May I concentrate not on changing others but on changing myself. Help me to realize that each day I can start fresh as a new person.

On some days you might write more than on other days, and that's okay. You might find it helpful to end each entry with a short prayer for the day, such as one of these:

Take my hand, Lord Jesus, and lead me through this day.

Help me look to you, God, when I face the problems of this day.

I place the concerns of my loved ones in your hands today, Lord.

Help me to be at peace within, O God, no matter how busy this day may be.

Remember, there's no right or wrong way to journal. Journaling is a very individual and private matter—although some couples receive great spiritual encouragement from sharing their writings. Be sure to talk about whether you will share your journals with each other, and then honor your agreement.

When can you set aside time each day for your devotional quiet time? Some couples have their devotions at night, because they are too rushed in the morning. Nighttime devotions are a good way to put the events of the day in perspective and get ready for the next day. Others prefer to have their quiet time in the morning with that first cup of coffee or orange juice as they read from the Bible or devotional materials, write in their journals, and pray. It's a wonderful way to start the day! In either case, sustaining a regular quiet time requires quite a bit of discipline, especially if you have children to care for. What, then, can you do?

You might try getting up fifteen or twenty minutes earlier—or going to bed fifteen or twenty minutes later. At first, this may be very hard to do, especially if you are getting up early or going to bed late as it is. If, however, you will make the commitment to try it for one week, or preferably, one month (it takes thirty days to form a habit), you just may discover that it changes your whole day—or life! Be careful not to resent having to get up early or go to bed late, or your quiet time will lose its effectiveness.

Another option is to have your quiet time sometime during the day—during a lunch break, the children's nap, or some other time. Be creative! Of course, few couples will be able to do this together during the day; but if a separate quiet time is your only option, remember that having a separate quiet time is better than having no quiet time! You might be amazed at how much even separate devotions will help your marriage!

Try not to be discouraged if you don't have time for your daily quiet time now and then. Likewise, you may not have time to write in your journal every day—and that's okay. Many people start and stop the discipline of a regular quiet time before it becomes a habit. The important thing is to establish a routine and try to be consistent. Ask God to help you become disciplined with your quiet time, and expect it to happen!

Anticipating Times of Change and Crisis: Transplanting and Fertilizing for New Growth

The label on the Miracle Grow plant fertilizer includes these words: "Ideal for transplanting." Just as a plant that has been transplanted needs extra tender loving care, so your marriage needs special care before, during, and after times of change and crisis. Whether your family is moving to another city—which actually is a "transplanting" of the family—is having money problems, is dealing with illness in the family, or is experiencing some other crisis or change, the "health" of your marriage plays an important role in determining whether you and your family will "survive and thrive." As we've said, a healthy marriage requires deep spiritual roots and adequate care and nurture. Obviously, you are better prepared to handle the inevitable times of change and crisis if you attend to these things not only *during* but well *before* difficult situations occur.

We see in the life of Jesus how he prepared his closest friends, the disciples, for a major change in their lives—a time when he no longer would be with them. He told them not to be afraid (John 14) but to grow in new ways, even in the midst of adjusting to loss and facing unknowns. Likewise, from the cross he spoke to his mother and the disciple named John, telling them to care for each other. His mother, who had been strong in her faith through the years, somehow endured all the pain and sorrow of that poignant scene, after which John took her to his home in a spirit of loving, protective care. If a similar need were to arise in your family at some time, would you be prepared to respond?

In addition to nurturing your faith and your relationship with each other, being adequately prepared for change and crisis involves the willingness to talk openly and honestly about some things that you might think are "depressing" or difficult to discuss. Take time now to think about the changes or crises you already have experienced as a couple and/or family and those that you think you might experience in the future. Complete the following sentences as you talk together.

Talking About Times of Change and Crisis

▲ The changes or crises we have experienced in the past include

_____

_____

▲ During those times, our faith _____

_____

▲ We helped each other through those times by _____

_____

▲ In the future, we might experience changes or crises such as _____

_____

▲ _____ would help us to be prepared for those times.

▲ A crisis may occur when one of us hurts the other. How do we forgive each other? As God forgives us? Can we each understand the difficulty for the other at such a time? We feel we can forgive and talk about little or big hurts by

_____

_____ .

▲ If we were to move, I would feel _____

_____

▲ When _____ dies, I will need you to _____

_____

(listen to me, hold me when I cry, understand my sadness, etc.)

▲ It is especially difficult to think of you being very ill, because _____

_____

▲ I would handle your illness by _____
(praying, getting support from family and friends, loving you more, caring for you, etc.)

How can you nurture your marriage and your relationship to God during these and other times of change and crisis? There are many different ways to cope with change and confront crises. One way is to practice forgiveness.

Practicing Forgiveness: Staying "Water Soluble"

Just as the nutrients in Miracle Grow dissolve in water, so should you learn to "dissolve" the disagreements, mistakes, and annoyances of your marriage—both small and big. How? By practicing forgiveness—one of the most important ways to nurture your marriage.

Forgiveness is a key to growth in marriage. It involves "asking and receiving"—asking to be forgiven and receiving forgiveness from the one who has been hurt by word or action. Forgiveness between a husband and wife means giving oneself again to the other in an expanded expression of unconditional love.

Forgiveness is a theme of Jesus' teachings. He told his disciples that there is no limit to the number of times we should forgive one another. One of the best examples of forgiveness in a marriage is the love of Hosea for his wife Gomer. Even though Gomer had an affair with another man, Hosea forgave her. Perhaps he had not been perfect, either, in his role as husband, but his willingness to forgive was the key to uniting them again in love.

It is difficult to forgive in an extreme situation such as the one in which Hosea found himself, but *it is possible*. It also is difficult for the one who has been hurt to learn to trust the other person again, but this too gradually can change, and a relationship of trust can be reestablished. Of course, it is essential that the one who has done something to hurt the other must change— refuse to continue the action or actions that caused the break in the marriage relationship. In time, a marriage can be rebuilt—and become even stronger. Like a physical wound, a wounded marriage eventually can heal, though it may be tender for a long time.

Hosea says that this is the way it is between God and us; God is always willing to forgive. Likewise, as husbands and wives, we must be willing to forgive each other.

Generally speaking, the bigger or more obvious the sin or annoyance, the quicker we are to realize the need for forgiveness. Yet often it is the smaller or less obvious sins and annoyances that, without forgiveness, can erode a marriage. Some classic examples of "little sins" and "little annoyances" that husbands and wives often complain about are telling white lies, keeping secrets (hiding something), complaining or whining, focusing on the negative, leaving the cap off the toothpaste tube, being late, leaving a pile of dirty clothes on the floor, forgetting to take out the trash or do some other chore, making too much noise and waking the other up, "channel surfing" with the remote control, and being disorganized—or overly organized. Although minor and seemingly insignificant, some of these behaviors and habits can cause great damage to a relationship if ignored. They are easily "dissolved," however, when a husband and wife are willing to talk about them, ask each other for forgiveness, accept each other unconditionally, and evaluate the importance of making any changes. When we know we are forgiven, most of us try to please our partner and not continue to do those things that irritate, annoy, or hurt.

Perhaps, however, you've heard someone say, "Well, that's just the way I am. I can't change"; or "You have to take the bad with the good"; or "If you don't like the way I am, too bad." The truth is, if we really love someone, we should be willing to make changes that not only will make that person happy but will improve our relationship. Though this is not always easy, it is possible through open communication, negotiation, and compromise—all of which help a marriage to grow.

Resiliency is an important factor in your ability to "dissolve" the annoying behaviors of your relationship with unconditional forgiveness—whether they be yours or those of your spouse. How resilient are you? Are you able to let truly insignificant annoyances "bounce off" you? Are you able to accept and forgive your spouse—without "keeping score"? Are you able to "bounce back" after hearing complaints or criticism, without harboring hurt feelings or resentment? If a complaint or criticism is valid, are you willing to ask for forgiveness and try to change?

Keep the following "resiliency questions" on hand and refer to them whenever something is causing friction between you and your spouse. (They're also helpful in dealing with problems in other relationships.)

Resiliency Questions

1. Is the criticism or complaint true? (Are you sloppy, always late, other? Some criticisms or complaints may be untrue. Consider how often you've heard the complaint, and whether you have heard similar comments from more than one person. Most often, there is at least some validity to the criticisms our spouses share with us.)
2. If it is true, am I willing to change? (If a complaint or criticism is valid and is now causing or could eventually cause a problem in your marriage, it is *always* important to consider changing your habit or behavior if at all possible.)
3. Whose problem is it? (It's your problem if you're at fault, or if there's something you really need to change. It may be, however, that the other person is being more critical than necessary or warranted.) If something is really bothering me or the other person but a change isn't warranted, whose problem is it? (Remember that a marriage is different from other relationships. If something is bothering you or your spouse, then your relationship *will* be affected—negatively, if you choose to do nothing about it.) Can we talk about this together?
4. How long am I going to let "it" bother me? (Ask yourself what steps you need to take to resolve this potential threat to your relationship. Do you need to seek forgiveness? Grant forgiveness? Make a change? Ask the other person to make a change? Accept "it" and let it "bounce off"? Resiliency also means to bounce back from a hurtful situation.)

If you have some difficulties now or in the future, try to get through the crisis by talking together, holding hands, and kneeling as you say a prayer something like this:

Help us, O Lord, during this time of _____
(e.g., change, sadness, difficulty in our marriage or our work,
illness) to_____.

At all times in your marriage, remember that the idea is always to try to change a habit or behavior that bothers your spouse—if it is a valid criticism or an obstacle in your relationship—and then bounce back from any criticism or hurt feelings that may have come between you. If you can go to bed each night without any anger between you, forgiving each other and affirming your love, you will nurture and nourish your marriage tremendously!

4. Celebrating Our Life Together and Giving Thanks for Growth

Albert Einstein once said, "There are only two ways to live our lives: as though nothing is a miracle or as though everything is a miracle." How true. Life itself is a miracle: the beauty and wonder of the human body and mind, of relationships with friends and family, of the love between you and your mate, and—the greatest miracle of all—of God's gift of love and grace through Jesus Christ. Do you recognize and give thanks for these and other "miracles" in your life?

Being grateful is one of the most important ways we can grow as individuals and as couples. When we express appreciation and celebrate together blessings we receive from God and gifts we receive from each other, something happens inside us. It's like a new leaf opening on a plant or flower bud bursting into bloom, as the feeling of thankfulness bursts open within us, bringing joy and beauty to our lives. Even little expressions of joy and praise can do wonders for a marriage, producing more growth than imaginable. Every couple has the constant need to reflect together on the goodness of life, even in the midst of tough times, and then to be thankful—to let the feeling of joy be expressed.

There are countless ways to cultivate a sense of joy and celebration in your lives and your marriage. Here are just a few ideas to get you started:

1. Give yourselves five minutes to list everything you love about your partner. Then share your lists and talk about them.
2. Work together to list all the occasions, both big and small, that you can celebrate together—as well as with other family members—birthdays, anniversaries, holidays, children's events/accomplishments, your own accomplishments, vacations, extended family celebrations, and so forth. Mark on your calendar any that you can, and plan to celebrate them! Remember, a celebration doesn't have to be time-consuming, elaborate, or expensive to be meaningful and fun!
3. Talk about simple ways you can celebrate more often. Eating out at a favorite fast-food restaurant? Picking or buying a simple flower? Preparing a special dish? Try to think of as many ways as you can to celebrate the "now," the present moment.
4. Show your appreciation to your spouse each day by saying something nice or expressing your appreciation for something specific.
5. Thank God individually and together for specific guidance and blessings you have received in unexpected ways or at unexpected times. Make this a regular habit!

6. Keep a list of everything you are thankful for, and continually add to it.
7. Take time each day to read something inspirational.
8. Make a record in a notebook of your insights, dreams, feelings, and what you have learned in your life journey.
9. Don't hesitate to call your pastor or a professional counselor if you need help renewing your mind or spirit.
10. Relax as you listen to the type of music that renews your spirit—whether it be hymns, praise music, contemporary Christian, classical, or something else.

Begin today to celebrate life—especially your life together. You may be amazed by the results!

Remember, if you want your marriage to continue growing, you must care for it lovingly and joyfully, as a gardener cares for the plants and flowers in a garden. By nurturing your marriage and giving careful attention to the spiritual roots that feed it, your marriage not only will grow but also will produce beautiful blossoms. Express your commitment to making this happen by putting a check beside those spiritual goals that you will strive to achieve.

Spiritual Goals

Wife	Husband	
——	——	I/we will try to set aside ten to twenty minutes each day for a daily quiet time with God.
——	——	I/we will regularly *participate* with a community of believers in worship.
——	——	I will develop my gifts for helping others through the gifts of my time, service, money, and possessions.
——	——	I will try to forgive myself and others, realizing that God forgives me.
——	——	I will continually try to grow in my relationship with God and my relationship with my partner.

Other goals:

Seal your commitment with this prayer, or one of your own:

God, help us to draw closer to you and your Spirit, so that we may realize how we can nurture and "grow" our marriage. Amen.

10. THE ONGOING JOURNEY

▼

As you begin this chapter

▲ place an object before you to symbolize your continuing journey through life together, a toy car or train, a suitcase or backpack, car keys, or something else.

▲ consider spending a day away from home at a nearby hotel, retreat center, or park—where you can look more objectively at your goals for the future.

1. Marriage Is a Journey

Devotional Thought: "The LORD, your God, is in your midst . . . he will renew you in his love" (Zephaniah 3:17*a, c*).

If you seek God's direction for your life together, God will renew your love and your marriage, giving you new life.

Prayer: God of love, give us a renewing love, and help us plan for the future in the Spirit of your Son, Jesus Christ, who showed us the way to love. Amen.

Marriage is a journey, and the way you travel on this journey—as individuals and as a couple—is as important as reaching your "destination." It is essential to make each other feel loved, respected, and cherished along the way. After all, you wouldn't want to make the trip with someone you did not enjoy being with, would you? If you travel lovingly and wisely, your marriage journey can be an enjoyable and rewarding experience.

As you journey together, it is helpful to have a "road map" before you. As we've explored previously, setting goals—for yourselves, your relationship, your children, your work, and every area of your lives—helps you look toward the future with purpose and determination. If you do this prayerfully, seeking God's guidance, God will renew your marriage again and again!

Before you begin looking at your "road map" together, take a few minutes to review three key "road signs" or goals that should be part of every married couple's journey. Though we have explored each of these in previous chapters, their importance to the future success of your marriage cannot be overemphasized.

1. We will strive to be as one, acknowledging that we also are unique individuals.

Before making any trip, you make choices about who will travel with you. After all, not everyone who might go with you will fit into the car! Likewise, the marriage journey requires that you leave others behind as you embark on your life adventure together. Matthew 19:5 reminds us that a man and woman must leave their families and be joined together as one.

Certainly it is good to have the support and love of your families of origin, but after marriage, your first loyalty is to your spouse. Some couples are so "enmeshed" with their original families that they do not spend enough time alone together or establish their own traditions. Such couples often communicate with and confide in other family members more than they do with each other—perhaps even about problems or concerns that should be shared only with each other and, in some cases, with a pastor or counselor. This may cause what is referred to as a relationship triangle, in which a son or daughter tells "secrets" to a parent rather than talking with his or her spouse.

Sometimes the parent and son or daughter even "take sides" against his or her mate. These destructive patterns prevent a couple from experiencing the unity that God intends for marriage and, ultimately, cause them—whether knowingly or unknowingly—to draw farther and farther apart. In some situations, the circle of love between a couple can "break," causing pain and feelings of rejection not only for themselves but also for their children. Such couples often are unable to reconcile and heal their relationship without the help of a pastor or marriage counselor.

The scriptures tell us that couples are to "leave" their parents and "cling" to each other. Being "best friends" with each other is one of the most important ways to ensure an enduring, loving relationship through the years.

Did you light a unity candle at your wedding? This is a common practice in many wedding ceremonies. Usually, the mothers of the bride and groom each light a single candle on either side of a large candle. Then, during the ceremony, the bride and groom use the side candles to light the center unity candle, symbolizing the uniting of their lives. In past years, couples would extinguish the side candles after lighting the center candle. Today, many couples leave these candles burning, acknowledging that they are unique individuals as well as united as a couple.

One of the most important goals for every married couple is striving to achieve unity—togetherness—while retaining their individuality. The best way to express this ideal is this: two individuals who are interdependent. Each person is an individual, as well as part of the whole, the circle of love.

Sometimes a couple begins marriage with one person being more dependent than the other. At first this may seem to be ideal, with one looking to the other to make decisions, to be the one "in control" or in charge. As the years go by, however, this relationship often changes. The one who has been dependent grows, becoming more and more independent and secure—perhaps because of security gained from the love of the other person. This independence, though it generally comes gradually, may be difficult for the one who has been the "leader" in the marriage. In other marriages, on the other hand, the "leader," who once liked having someone look to him or her for decision making, can grow tired or even resentful of this responsibility as years go by. In either situation, couples must continually remind themselves that God has created each of us as individual creations, intending us to live as fully as we can with our unique gifts and to share together as husband and wife in the beautiful relationship of love, *with God leading the way* in the journey of marriage.

In summary, a marriage is healthy when there is the right balance for growth—as individuals and as a couple.

2. We will nurture our relationship and keep it strong, giving it the time and loving attention it deserves, while striving to maintain balance in our lives.

As we've mentioned throughout this book, spending time together and nurturing every aspect of your relationship, including physical intimacy, is vital to the health of your marriage. The challenge is giving your relationship adequate attention and care while fulfilling your many other responsibilities. When children come along, it becomes particularly challenging and yet even more important to maintain this intimacy and balance. Remember, the best gift you can give to your children is your own strong marriage relationship.

In addition to spending time together and keeping the spark of romantic love burning, practicing healthy communication on a regular basis is another important way to develop and maintain a close relationship with your spouse. Being able to talk openly and honestly about your hurts, concerns, conflicts, and anger—without resentment or bitterness—should be a continuing priority in your marriage. Not only will your efforts to nurture your relationship enrich your marriage; they also will help to carry you and your family through any difficult times you may experience, such as illness, money problems, or other unpredictable crises.

3. We will make laughter and humor a part of our lives, always keeping things in proper perspective.

Laughter and humor are important requirements for a happy, healthy marriage. They also help to make the marriage journey infinitely more enjoyable! Those couples who enjoy each other's company and laugh together regularly are more likely to remain "traveling companions" than those who are always serious and somber, who consider their life together to be boring or burdensome, rather than joyful and exciting.

Being able to laugh at the absurdities in your daily lives, as well as at yourselves, helps you to keep life in perspective. When you laugh *with* each other—not *at* each other—you remind each other that life is a precious gift to be enjoyed and cherished, even when things don't "go your way." Laughter helps to heal your wounds, restore your optimism, and give you the energy you need to make it through even the most difficult times. Laughter actually strengthens your marriage!

2. A Road Map for Your Journey

Meet Mike and Laurie, who have lived in the Midwest since they were married. In fact, the Midwest was "home" for each of them before they were married. Now they are celebrating their first decade together. Their years together have been good ones. Both have built rewarding careers and have had good health—with the exception of Mike's appendectomy last year, which made them cancel their vacation plans. Money has never been a problem, although they would not describe themselves as affluent. Church has been a central focus in their expression of faith and their outreach to others, and they have become increasingly involved in community projects.

For the first six years of their marriage, there were just the two of them. During the past four years, they have been blessed with the arrival of Julie, their daughter and the delight of their lives. They have enjoyed watching her grow and have surrounded her with love.

Mike and Laurie have been alone for a few days, celebrating their tenth anniversary in a cabin beside a like in the Ozarks. The cabin belongs to Laurie's parents and is used by all the members of Laurie's family at different times. This trip has been the best ever for Laurie and Mike. They've enjoyed being together without any agenda other than relaxing, talking, walking, reading, and sharing their love.

It is their last night in the cabin; tomorrow morning they will be going home. As they sit together on the couch beside the window, they watch the sun set over the lake. On the table in front of them is a small bouquet of wildflowers that Mike picked for Laurie and a candle that they have lit each night. One of Laurie's "traditions" is to take a candle with them every time they are away. Also on the table is a road map—spread out so that they may plan a different route for their trip home.

Read their conversation as if you are Laurie and Mike.

Mike: This is the best anniversary ever, Laurie, and it hardly cost anything!

Laurie: Maybe that's because it brings back so many good memories of other times we've had here together—all the way back to that first time we were here with my parents. We weren't even married then.

Mike: I sure remember that time. You were in one bedroom, your parents were in the other, and I slept out here on the couch! All night I kept thinking about the day when I'd be sharing the same bed with you here. We've had a lot of those times since then—and it sure beats sleeping on the couch!

Laurie: I remember the first time we brought Julie with us. She loved the water, and we had so much fun with her on that little inflatable raft! I hope she's doing all right.

Mike: We just talked to her yesterday, honey! You know she's having a ball. She loves being with Grandpa and Grandma on the farm.

Laurie: I hope we can always come to this place, so she can enjoy the same kinds of things I enjoyed as a kid when we would come here. (Pauses for a moment.) But what about your job offer in Los Angeles? That would take us so far away.

Mike: I don't think it's realistic for us to consider, Laurie. It sounded so good at first, and I know it's a lot more money; but you'd have to leave your job too and there's so much adjustment with that kind of move—so far away from the rest of our family. Besides, LA has so much traffic and smog, and housing is a lot more expensive.

Laurie: But it would be a good career move for you. Isn't that what most career counselors would advise? And we have to keep in mind that I may not want to have a job, especially if we have another child.

Mike: I know. I want us to have another baby too, but maybe that's even more reason for us to stay where we are—where our roots are, where we feel secure.

Laurie: Let's keep praying about it, and we can talk more on the way home.

Mike: Okay. You know, I've been looking at this map, and there's an interesting little town about midway that we've been wanting to explore. I bet it has some antique stores.

Laurie: And maybe a quaint little restaurant where we could eat lunch!

Mike: Sure. We're in no rush to get home. It's not that long a trip.

Laurie: (Laughing) Maybe some new scenery will give us some new insights about that job offer! Hey... (pauses) I was just thinking of something. We get out the map and carefully plan our route home, right? We ought to be just as intentional about planning *our future.*

Mike: What do you mean?

Laurie: Why don't we get two pieces of paper and write down where we want to be in five years from now—what our family will be like, where we'll be living, what we'll be doing, how we'll be spending our time and money—you know, something of a five-year plan?

Mike: Then what?

Laurie: Then we can talk about our goals and decide how we can combine them—or how we want to change them—in order to come up with a plan we both agree with. But first we should do it separately, without looking at each other's paper. What do you think?

Mike: You're always the teacher, aren't you? Okay, why not? But I need something to get me thinking—like a bowl of popcorn!

Laurie: Okay. You make the popcorn; it's in the cabinet over the stove, and there's some tea in the fridge. I'll get some paper and pens and write the different headings for our five-year plan. Who knows? Maybe this will become our anniversary tradition.

Mike: Maybe it will.

Take a look at Mike and Laurie's separate five-year plans. Note that some projections are more realistic than others; the "dream goals" are in parentheses. Discuss how you feel about Mike and Laurie's future. How could they combine some of these goals? Are they missing any important aspects of marriage? What is needed to make their plan complete? Do you think they should move to Los Angeles or stay in the Midwest? Why? What would you do?

Laurie and Mike's Five-Year Plans

Focus	Laurie	Mike
What will our family be like?	The three of us—plus a new baby!	Laurie, Julie, me, and more.
Where will we be living?	Los Angeles	Where we are now.
What will our home look like?	Ranch—3 bedrooms	(Indoor swimming pool added.)
What will we be doing?	I'll be substitute teaching; Mike will be in sales.	Me: same job; Laurie still teaching.
Any pets?	A kitten.	Puppy for the kids.
Amount in savings?	$10,000 for kids' college.	$30,00 for new home.
What will we do on Sundays?	Sunday school and church; spending time with kids.	Church; visiting relatives.
What will be our happiest times (when not working)?	Playing together as a family.	In bed together after kids are asleep.
How healthy will we be?	Good condition, keeping weight down with diet; regular checkups.	Great health in every way; both of us working out.
How will we celebrate our 15th anniversary?	(Mediterranean cruise! Followed by week in Paris.)	Quiet week at the lake together.

What will our goals be then?	Good savings program; plans for postgraduate degree for both of us (?); more time for prayer and meditation; being best parents we can be.	Having good retirement plan; buying a boat; expanded fitness plan; "family hobby" or activity.
Other dreams for the future:	Planing and caring for a beautiful flower garden; helping our children develop their special abilities and qualities ad a love for life!	Writing short stories or magazine articles; being a good dad (more relaxed); learning to fly a plane.

Now take time to think as objectively as possible about what goals your own five-year plan might include. Couples responding to one survey listed future goals such as living in a small town, writing a book, being there for children and grandchildren while they're growing up, taking a real vacation (not to visit family), traveling, and continuing to grow in faith together. Your goals may include some of these, or they may be very different. Before you begin, you might find it helpful to review the priorities you listed on pages 15-16 and the marriage inventory you completed on page 18.

Following the example of Laurie and Mike, complete your five-year plans separately at first. Make a copy of the following grid, or take turns completing it, covering the responses of your partner as necessary. Do not allow this to be a lengthy process. Simply write down the first thoughts you have so that you will be more likely to discuss them without a defensive attitude.

Our Five-Year Plan

Focus	Wife	Husband
What will our family be like? (names and ages)		
Where will we be living?		
What will our home look like? (if same home, note any changes)		
What will we be doing? (work and/or daily experiences)		

Any pets?

Gross annual income?

Amount in savings? (note %
earmarked for specific
purposes)

What will we do on
Sundays?

What will be our happiest
times (when not working)?

How healthy will we be?

How will we celebrate our
anniversary?

What will our goals be then?

Other dreams for the future:

Enjoy a snack together as you share and discuss your responses, try to be as open to your mate's ideas as possible—whether they be realistic goals or "off the wall" dreams. Then choose which ones you think should be included in your goals for the next five years. Do this by simply circling those that you agree upon, realizing that if you want your five-year plan to be successful, you must begin the journey with these "destinations" on your "road map."

Agree to review your five-year plan every six months, giving yourselves ten "check points" along your journey. Schedule your six-month checkups just as you would schedule appointments with your dentist or physician. Allow a full afternoon or evening (away from the children, if you have any) for each. Make these checkups a priority, marking the date and time for each on all of your calendars! (Most couples have more than one.) You also

Do-It-Yourself Marriage Enrichment

might want to write yourself a reminder to stick it to the refrigerator one week in advance. Allow your checkup times to be fun and creative—not something you feel you *have* to do, but something you *want* to do!

3. Making Choices and Commitments as You Journey Together

Devotional Thought: "Choose this day whom you will serve" (Joshua 24:15).

Read the following aloud:

As We Begin Each Day

Together: Here we are. Even as night always comes, so also a new morning arrives fresh with hope, as the sun touches the earth. The choice is ours of how to live each day. How will we relate to each other and those around us?

Wife: We choose to be patient, especially at times when it seems things are not going our way—when we are frustrated and irritated, perhaps from events of the day or with each other for little or not-so-little reasons.

Husband: We choose to be kind to each other in words and actions, even as we are with others throughout the day.

Wife: We choose to be filled with hope and a positive outlook when discouraged or experiencing difficulties as we approach tasks and problems of the day or our ongoing lives.

Husband: We will forgive and allow ourselves to be forgiven when we are hurt, or hurt someone else, remembering, we can choose to be different, as God forgives us.

Wife: We will speak gently and with self-control, yet with the confidence of our beliefs and values when discussing issues or making decisions, realizing compromise and understanding are always essential.

Husband: We will take time to listen and seek to understand each other without being judgmental or critical even as we also relate to others.

Wife: We will reach out in kindness to those who mistreat us, and will touch with love the poor, sick, sad and lonely, as God reaches out to us.

Together: We choose to walk through the hours of this day with an awareness that God's love surrounds us, and as we place our heads on our pillows tonight, we will thank God for guiding us. If we have failed in any way, we know that we can choose to live better tomorrow as a new dawn arrives.

Remember that each day is a choice—*your choice.* Determine how you will spend your time, how you will express your feelings, and how you will make choices, always looking to God for guidance. A five-year plan or "road map" for your marriage is of little value unless you live each day with a sense of adventure and with commitment to God and to each other, striving to make each day the best it can be.

As you read the following commitment checklist (one is provided for each of you), you will note that these are summary statements of the ideas presented throughout this book. Since discussing these ideas previously, perhaps you have conscientiously tried to implement or improve on them in your marriage. Or perhaps there are some that need your special attention. Put a checkmark beside those commitments that you will make part of your marriage journey, beginning today! (You may want to photocopy these prior to completing them so that you can keep them personally afterward.)

"Her" Commitment Checklist

I will try to do the following in our future marriage journey together:

_____   Encourage my partner more.

_____   Listen more attentively to what my partner is saying.

_____   Think of creative ways to "keep the spark alive," such as _____

          _____

_____   Try to be a better parent by _____

          _____

_____   Talk in a caring, calm way when I am upset.

_____   Say "I'm sorry" when I should.

_____   Take the following steps to grow more spiritually: _____

          _____

_____   Set regular times for physical exercise.

_____   Share household responsibilities with my partner.

_____   Schedule regular medical checkups and encourage my partner to do the same.

_____   Plan mini-vacations or a "full-blown" annual get-away with my partner only.

_____ Set aside time on a weekly basis to review our schedule and special needs.

_____ Worship regularly and participate as a couple/family in outreach efforts.

_____ Talk openly with my partner about things that may be bothering me, such as _____

_____

_____ Discuss financial concerns creatively, agreeing how much we will give and save.

_____ Say "I love you" in new ways, rather than allowing expressions to be routine.

_____ Other commitments I will make so that our marriage journey can be the best it can be:

"His" Commitment Checklist

I will try to do the following in our future marriage journey together:

_____ Encourage my partner more.

_____ Listen more attentively to what my partner is saying.

_____ Think of creative ways to "keep the spark alive," such as _____

_____

_____ Try to be a better parent by _____

_____

_____ Talk in a caring, calm way when I am upset.

_____ Say "I'm sorry" when I should.

_____ Take the following steps to grow more spiritually: _____

_____

_____ Set regular times for physical exercise.

_____ Share household responsibilities with my partner.

_____ Schedule regular medical checkups and encourage my partner to do the same.

_____ Plan mini-vacations or a "full-blown" annual get-away with my partner only.

_____ Set aside time on a weekly basis to review our schedule and special needs.

_____ Worship regularly and participate as a couple/family in outreach efforts.

_____ Talk openly with my partner about things that may be bothering me, such as _____

_____.

_____ Discuss financial concerns creatively, agreeing how much we will give and save.

_____ Say "I love you" in new ways, rather than allowing expressions to be routine.

_____ Other commitments I will make so that our marriage journey can be the best it can be:

Share your commitment checklists with each other, realizing that these are ongoing, working documents, intended to serve as expressions of your commitment to each other as well as to the total adventure of marriage. Keep your own checklist as a reminder of how you plan to live as a partner in marriage—as the best husband or wife you can be. Perhaps you can keep your list in a special place where you will see it frequently.

4. A Covenant to Sign and a Letter to Send

A covenant is an agreement shared between the two of you in a spirit of love and trust. It is quite different from a contract, which is more legalistic in form. When you make a covenant with each other, you pledge your best possible effort to fulfill what you both want to achieve together.

The following covenant combines and summarizes many of the commitments described in this book. It serves as an ongoing reminder of your plan to keep your marriage vital and vibrant. In many ways, it complements and enhances the covenant you shared on your wedding day through the vows you repeated to each other. You may want to keep this covenant as part of this book, or cut it out and tape it to the inside of your Bible, or even frame it and hang it in a special place.

Our Covenant of Love and Commitment

We agree to share a devotional time each day, if possible, and to take time to pray together.

We agree to talk together on a weekly basis about all the things we need to discuss—including our plans, finances, children, work, and simply how we feel about life.

We agree to spend time alone together, preferably on a "date," every other week or once a month—even if we're only able to share a cup of coffee or tea.

We agree to take care of our physical bodies, recognizing them as the temple of God; we each will give attention to our own health and strength, as well as the health and strength of our partner.

We agree to be the best parents we can possibly be (if we have children), or to help care for other children (if we have no children of our own).

We agree to share what we have with others who are unable to provide for their daily needs, and to lend our time and effort as a couple to help meet such needs.

We agree to express our love for each other in words; in touch, embraces, and physical intimacy; and in creative expressions of love and appreciation.

We agree always to be thankful to God and to ask for guidance and blessing as God's Spirit provides courage and hope on the journey that awaits us.

_____   _____
        signature   signature

            _____
                    date

Now write a letter to your mate, expressing your love for him or her. Use the circle of love stationery provided on pages 167 and 168, or your own personal stationery, if you prefer. Write today's date at the top of your letter, put it in an envelope and seal it, write your mate's name and your home address on the envelope, and keep it in a safe place until you are ready to mail it—on an ordinary day when it will be a special surprise, or a special day such as his or her birthday or your anniversary.

As you conclude this time together and come to the end of your "marriage enrichment workshop," remember that the circle of love is a circle in which you share and explore and give and receive—with thankful hearts and unlimited possibilities for the future. Read the following poem together as a celebration of what has been and a promise of what is yet to be.

Our Circle of Love*

We've come together to understand
The journey of marriage—hand in hand.
We shared our love in a wedding vow,
And we reaffirm it now.

So let us remember the years gone by,
The times we've laughed, the times we've cried,
And thank our God whose promise is true
As our covenant we now renew.

As we look into each other's eyes,
There's a spark of love that never dies.
Let words convey what's in the heart,
Our love that was there from the start.

(Refrain)
This, this is the circle of love,
Blessed by God around and above.
So much to live, and so much to give,
Within our circle of love.

*This poem can be sung to the tune of "Greensleeves."

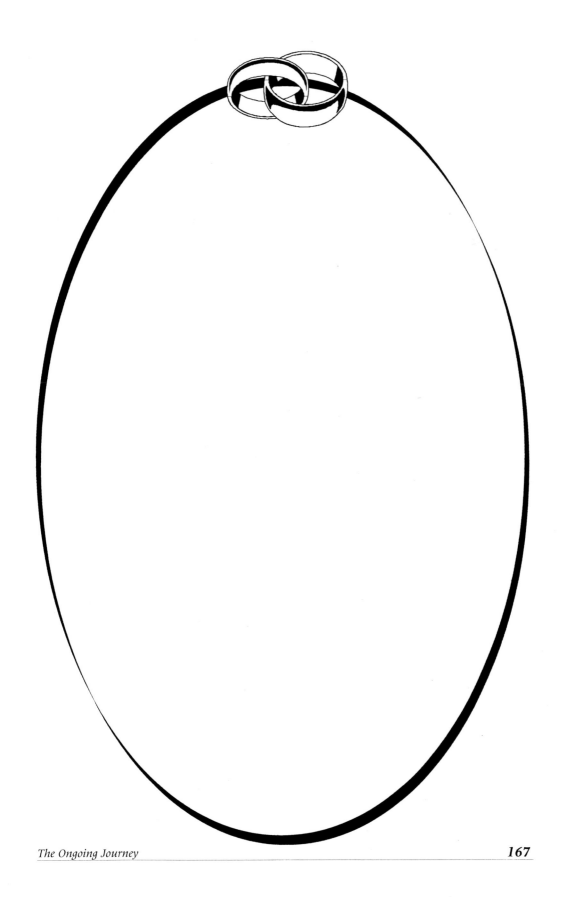

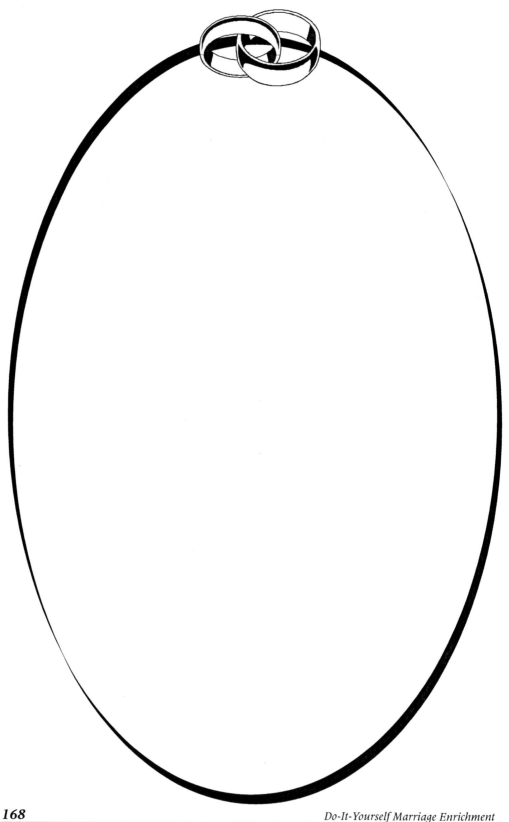

TEN STEPS FOR SOLVING PROBLEMS

Every couple has differences, but healthy couples find ways to solve these problems in the best way. They encourage and utilize open expression. The following steps may be helpful as you consider a problem you face.

1. Set a date, time, and place for both of you to meet within a week or two. Allow at least thirty minutes, but no more than one hour.

   Meeting Date: _____

   Time: _____

   Place: _____

2. Identify one important issue or problem you would like to resolve.

   _____

   _____

3. In what ways are each of you contributing to this problem? Without blaming each other, list the things each of you do that have not helped to resolve the problem (e.g., one of your saying, "I know I'm right," getting angry rather than discussing the problem).

   Husband: Wife:

   _____   _____

   _____   _____

   _____   _____

4. List past attempts to resolve this issue (e.g., discussing each year whether to buy a house or have a baby without coming to an agreement; minor disagreements; etc.)

   _____

   _____

   _____

5. Brainstorm new ideas and possible solutions, even if some of them sound "way out." Do not discuss, criticize, or judge any ideas now. Let yourselves have fun!

The Ongoing Journey   **169**

_____

_____

_____

_____

6. Now discuss each of these possible solutions. Try to be objective, talk calmly, listen to each other, and remain open to new possibilities. Ask yourselves if any of these ideas can resolve the disagreement.

7. After each of you has expressed your feelings, select one solution that you both agree to try.

Trial Solution: _____

_____

Place: _____

8. Agree how you will work toward this solution. Be as specific as possible.

_____

_____

9. Set a date, time, and place for another meeting within the next week to discuss your progress.

Meeting Date: _____
Time: _____
Place: _____

10. Be especially tender and attentive to each other after this first meeting, being careful to notice each other's positive efforts and contributions to making the solution work and taking time to give each other praise.

Future Meetings

• At your next meeting, discuss your progress. Has the trial solution worked? If not, try a different one and set a date, time, and place for another meeting within one week.

• Try to plan weekly meetings when you can discuss schedules and/or problems and simply talk together. Frequently couples do not have enough "objective time" to look at issues together.

The Ten Steps for Resolving Couple Conflict is a component in the PREPARE/ENRICH Program that was developed by Dr. David H. Olson, who is Professor, Family Social Science, University of Minnesota, St. Paul, Minnesota.

FOR FURTHER READING

▼

Branden, Nathaniel, *The Psychology of Self-Esteem,* Bantam, New York, 1983.

Branden, Nathaniel, *How to Raise Your Self-Esteem,* Bantam, New York, 1988.

Briscoe, Stuart and Jill, *Marriage Matters!* Harold Shaw Publishers, Wheaton, Illinois, 1994.

Broderick, Carlfred, *Couples, How to Confront Problems and Maintain Loving Relationships,* Simon & Schuster, New York, 1979.

Burkett, Larry, *The Financial Planning Organizer,* The Christian Financial Concepts Series, Inc., Gainesville, Georgia, 1996.

Campbell, Ross, *How to Really Love Your Children,* Inspirational Press, Budget Book Service, Inc., New York, 1992.

Cohen, Susan and Daniel, *Teenage Stress,* Dell Publishing, Bantam Doubleday Dell Publishing Group, Inc., New York, 1984.

Curran, Dolores, *Stress and the Healthy Family,* Harper Collins, New York, 1987.

DeKruyter, Arthur, *Love Makes Life, Seeing God's Reflection in Everyday Relationships,* Tyndale House Publishers, 1981.

Dobson, James, *Life on the Edge,* Word Press, Dallas, Texas, 1995.

Eyre, Richard and Linda, *Three Steps to a Strong Family,* Simon & Schuster, New York, 1994.

Godek, Gregory, *1001 Ways to Be Romantic,* Casablanca Press, Inc., Weymouth, Mass., 1995.

Gray, John, *Men Are from Mars, Women Are from Venus,* HarperCollins, New York, 1994.

Helmering, Doris, *Happily Ever After,* Warner Communications Co., New York, 1986.

Hendrix, Harville, *Keeping the Love You Find,* Simon & Schuster, New York, 1992.

Hendrix, Harville, and Hunt, Helen, *The Couples Companion,* Simon & Schuster, New York, 1994.

Hudson, Kathi, *Raising Kids God's Way,* Crossway Book, Wheaton, Illinois, 1995.

Jones, Riki Robbins, *Negotiating Love,* Ballantine Books, New York, 1995.

Keirsey, David, and Bates, Marilyn, *Please Understand Me.* Prometheus Nemesis Book Co., Delmar, California, 1984.

Krueger, Caryl, *365 Ways to Love Your Child,* Abingdon Press, Nashville, 1994.

Lansky, Vicki, *101 Ways to Tell Your Children "I Love You,"* Contemporary Books, Chicago, Illinois, 1988.

Lauer, Jeanette and Robert, *For Better and Better: Building a Healthy Marriage for a Lifetime,* Dimensions for Living, Nashville, 1995.

Lauer, Jeanette and Robert, *Intimacy on the Run,* Dimensions for Living, Nashville, 1996.

Liontos, Lynn and Demetri, *The Good Couple Life,* Association of Couples for Marriage Enrichment, Inc., Winston-Salem, North Carolina, 1982.

Luecke, David, *Prescription for Marriage,* Relationship Institute, Columbia, Maryland, 1989.

Luecke, David, *The Relationship Manual,* The Relationship Institute, Columbia, Maryland, 1981.

Mace, David, *When the Honeymoon's Over,* Abingdon Press, Nashville, 1988.

Marriage Partnership Staff, *Couples' Devotional Bible,* New International Version, Zondervan Publishing House, 1994.

Page, Susan, *Now That I'm Married, Why Isn't Everything Perfect?* Dell Publishing, New York, 1995.

Palmer, Pat, and Froehner, Melissa, *Esteem,* Impact Publishers, San Luis Obispo, California, 1989.

Ramsey, Dave, *Financial Peace,* Lampo Press, New York, 1992.

Roth, Larry, *Living Cheap News,* Contemporary Books, Chicago, Illinois, 1996.

Smalley, Gary, and John Trent, *Love Is a Decision,* Word Publishing, Dallas, Texas, 1989.

Smalley, Gary, and Trent, John, *The Language of Love,* Focus on Family Publishing, Pomona, California, 1991.

Smedes, Lewis, *The Art of Forgiving,* Moorings, Nashville, 1996.

Sose, Bonnie and Holly, *Designed by God So I Must Be Special,* Character Builders for Kids, Winter Park, Florida, 1988.

St. James, Elaine, *Inner Simplicity,* Hyperion, New York, 1995.

St. James, Elaine, *Simplify Your Life,* Hyperion, New York, 1994.

Wallerstein, Judith and Blakeslee, Sandra, *The Good Marriage,* Warner Books, Houghton Mifflin Co., New York, 1995.

Wanner, Donna Ternes, *Just for Me—The Self-Esteem and Wellness Guide for Girls,* Spiritseeker Publishing, Inc., Fargo, North Dakota, 1994.

Whitehead, Evelyn and James, *Marrying Well, Possibilities in Christian Marriage Today,* Doubleday, Garden City, New York, 1981.